DOMINATE THE GAME

Jennifer A. Garrett

Kevin,
You are always making moves and making things happen! Keep going against the grain and dominating the game!!

Jennifer A. Garrett

DOMINATE THE GAME

Jennifer A. Garrett

Copyright © 2022 by Jennifer A. Garrett

Printed and Electronic Versions
ISBN Paperback 978-1-956353-31-0
ISBN Hardback 978-956353-32-7
ISBN eBook 978-1-956353-33-4
(Jennifer A. Garrett/Motivation Champs)

The book was printed
in the United States of America.

To order additional copies or bulk order contact the publisher, Motivation Champs Publishing. www.motivationchamps.com

TESTIMONIALS

"Jen is a fighter. A detail-oriented and an extremely intelligent person that anyone would want in their corner. Her vast knowledge and transferable skill set allows her to have excellent rapport with people of all ages and different walks of life. She is honest, organized, and exceptional at being innovative to help those in need. You'll find out in *Dominate the Game* that Jen is trustworthy, compassionate, and willing to go above & beyond in her love of service for others."

—Chris Leak, University of Florida & Professional Football Quarterback, 2006 BCS National Champion

"Jennifer is exceptional at translating sports concepts into analogies and lessons that can help anyone to suit up, to show up, and to move the ball forward. Jennifer understands the trials and triumphs on the football field and she reveals so many valuable principles to help anyone reach that level in business and in life that they are looking to achieve."

—Tyrone P. Keys, 1985 Chicago Bears, Super Bowl XX Champion, Founder of All Sports Community Service

"Jen's writing and speaking style is the perfect match of passion meeting talent and depth. Her deep love of football and the way it's played allows her to understand it at a level missed by most of us. She then takes that wisdom and applies it to the business world to, in essence, give us the tools to build a Super Bowl caliber team."

—Andrew Coleman, President, GE Digital, Aviation

"I like to say that Jen has more degrees than a thermometer. But don't be fooled by the knowledge alone. With experience in so many 'rooms', Jen's military background makes her much like a professional athlete. She understands discipline, focus, preparation, and sacrifice. She's got lots of 'reps' in real life and real meaningful scenarios. *Dominate the Game* will help you grab some practical nuggets to apply now so that you too can make a greater impact!"

—*Rob Vaka, Athlete Mentor, Entrepreneur, People Connector*

"Jen is crushing it! She's a mother of five, business consultant, author, podcast host, and serves in the US military as an attorney. She is a true inspiration."

—*Bill Cartwright, University of San Francisco Basketball Player, NBA Player, NBA Coach, 5-time NBA Champion*

"I agree that life is about showing up. Jennifer continues to show up, inspire, and be a leader in everything she gets involved in ... Military service, business consulting, podcasts, and authoring books, including her latest book, *Dominate the Game*. I admire her continued persistence; she is a force."

—*Rob Thompson, Serial Entrepreneur & Former NFL and Disney Executive*

"Jen's unique take on connecting football to life lessons applies to almost any business or personal decision. She shares such great insights to help people move forward in her latest book, *Dominate the Game*."

—*Jim Duquette, Former GM for the NY Mets and Baltimore Orioles, MLB Front Office Executive, Baseball Analyst on MLB Network Radio, SNY, & Athletic*

CONTENTS

CHAPTER 1:
INTRODUCTION

"In life, be a participant, not a spectator."
—Lou Holtz

Boom! In a flash it's gone. Another year of your life has disappeared…525,600 minutes evaporated into thin air. Okay maybe that's a bit dramatic, but I had to get your attention.

You're familiar with the saying "time flies when you're having fun," but the reality is that's not the only reason time goes by quickly; sometimes we are just too dang busy trying to survive "the rat race" or navigate through life and time simply passes us by. Before you know it, you're wondering where it all went. Your children went from being babies to celebrating their fifth birthday to becoming a teenager to graduating high school in what feels like an instant. Yes, I'm still being dramatic, but parents, I know you can relate.

Even if you don't have kids, you can surely appreciate how time elapses surprisingly fast. One day you've graduated high school, the next it seems like you're walking across the stage getting your college degree, and then you're worrying about being a corporate professional or successful entrepreneur and how to traverse life, pay your rent or your mortgage, your phone bill, your cable (for those who still have cable), and those other darn utilities.

The thing about time, too, is that once it's spent, you can *never* get it back.

Take a moment and reflect on this past year. How many seconds, minutes, and hours did you spend on unnecessary activities, unproductive meetings, and inefficient processes, versus time spent truly living in your purpose and focused on the things that really mattered to you? I'm talking about everything…job-related, business matters, and personal stuff.

While this answer is different for each of us, for most, there will be a common theme: *I wish I had more time. I didn't get to focus on the things I wanted to. I was too busy with my job. Holy crap, I really didn't prioritize what I should have. What the heck did I get done this past year???*

Life is a journey you only get to experience once. Therefore, it's up to you to really make it count. I'm not just talking about the daring "yolo" stuff you see people wanting to do to be adventurous. It's about having the courage to leave your safe zone, to abandon the familiar and live the life that you want. It's about not limiting yourself. It's about dominating the game, showing up the right way, and creating a future self that you can be proud of.

Here's the thing. In the book of life, everyone has their own path. Do you want someone else to author your story, or do you want to be the one with the pen and paper? To put that in more modern terms, are you going to be the one on the computer typing the keystrokes for your story? However it gets written, don't let your narrative be dictated by others; rather write your own chapters and don't be afraid to turn the page and start a new one as needed. The point is, *take command and don't get comfortable.*

Something that I have learned throughout my life is that it is important to have the courage to live a life true to yourself, to be willing to go against the grain, and to not live the life others expect of you. There are times we will need to be spontaneous and crazy, play hard, take chances, leave our comfort zone, give it everything we've got, and do things others won't do to capture the meaningful moments in life and to make the most of each day. Live without limits and regret nothing.

It takes a daring person to live fiercely and without regrets. You can't be afraid to make mistakes, learn from them, and then move forward over and over and over again. That's how life should be.

When you're able to do this, embracing every opportunity and challenge for what they're worth, whether they intrigue you or frustrate you, the rewards are greater than any stumbles you may encounter along the way. They really are.

My journey has certainly proven that to me. In this book, I'll share with you some examples I personally had to face that tested me and shaped the road I am on now, getting to work with some of the world's most influential leaders and top-notch professional athletes. Remember that achieving greatness and living a meaningful and fulfilling life is about pushing boundaries and testing perceived limits.

Life is riddled with uncertainty. When faced with new situations, you can choose one of two options: you can be a player who is paralyzed by unknowns, or you can be a brave soul fearless of the vagueness you will face on the road ahead. Throughout this book, the principles covered will challenge you, pushing you to become confident in your ability to conquer any situation you may face in pursuit of your goals, ambitions, and dreams.

This book will help you minimize your fears and become comfortable with uncomfortable environments. Now, how you choose to suit up, show up, and play your game is entirely up to you. But I'm here to be that coach to keep you off the sideline, locked in and playing the game, ready to move the ball, and get you across your goal line.

Life will throw you curve balls, fast balls, tight spiral passes, and wobbly, undefined ones. If you are really trying to push yourself to that next level, uncertainty will be a common obstacle you will encounter. When these situations surface, don't be afraid of them. Instead, embrace them. Then keep moving forward and don't stop until the finish line is behind you.

People often say to me, "Jen, you're the busiest person I know."

Or "Jen, you have seven degrees! What? And how do you balance your five kids with everything else that you have going on?"

Or "Jen, how do you not lose your mind juggling everything? I don't know how you do it."

The answer to those two last questions might simply boil down to one thing: *I might be a little bit crazy.* That's a story for another day, though. But all joking aside, there are some things that I do to help me move the ball and make things happen.

Every day I choose to "suit up" with a mindset full of gratitude, one that appreciates being able to wake up and live another day. Each one is truly a gift.

Every day I choose to "show up" in the world with a smile on my face, not because my life is perfect, but because I appreciate the blessings that I have. I'm ready to bring positive energy and be a positive influence on those around me.

Every day I choose to "move the ball" and be fully present because life is too short to not make the most of each day. I want to live my life regretting nothing and never wondering *what if?*

Life is full of choices and every day you get to choose how you will suit up, show up, and whether you are going to move the ball. Ask yourself, what are your choices going to be? This book is structured in three parts and will give you tools, strategies, and principles to help you navigate through any situation and to win in life.

Something to always keep in mind is that people will look at you and judge you for where you are at today without knowing what you gave up, what you sacrificed, and what you did to get there. As the late Walter Payton said, "You have to fight for every single yard."

People reach out to me all the time telling me how "lucky" I am, how I get to live an amazing life, and how it's so much fun. But what they don't see is all the blood, sweat, tears, and more that went into building the Move the Ball brand. They don't see how I had to fight for every inch, just to get to another yard.

I remember the days when no one from football gave a damn about what I knew about the game—the game that I had fallen in love with at four years old and became a student of ever since. The game that has always been a huge part of my life.

I remember the disappointment, the heartache, and all the rejection (and yes there was plenty of it, which I'll share more about in this book).

I also remember the times when I told myself that I would always remember my worth and no matter how many people didn't care, didn't see my value, and flat out told me "No," that I would continue to push forward and "move the ball."

Sometimes you have to go after a dream and a vision that others don't see. All that matters is what you believe and that you are always willing to bet on yourself. You can't let others dial down your ambition because they are uncomfortable with the volume.

By the end of this book, I want you to stop asking for permission. Your life is 100% your responsibility. You get to choose how you show up to it and what you get done each day. I'm a firm believer in the importance of taking charge of your life and being that quarterback that moves the ball towards your goal line. You should always be writing a life story that you never want to stop reading.

Life is about being happy. You deserve to be happy. The first step is to develop your foundation and define who you are and what you want to become. Next, you need to create your plan. Last, you must take action, pressing forward to make your dreams a reality.

Life is a game where you must actively participate. This should not be a spectator sport. You've got to own it, then dominate it. Imagine you are inside a football stadium.

In my first book, *Move the Ball: How the Game of American Football Can Help You Achieve Your Life Goals*, I analogize your life to a football field, and you are the quarterback driving the plays. To succeed in life, some of the questions you must answer are as follows:

- *Are you where you currently want to be?*
- *Do you know what jersey you are wearing?*
- *Did you suit up with the right clothes on?*
- *Are you showing up and being where your feet are?*
- *What did you do today to move the ball?*

These are all important concepts we will examine throughout this book and more.

I consider myself to have been blessed with many opportunities, both professionally and personally. But just like everyone else, my life has had its share of challenges. For one, I started off my young adulthood as a teen single parent. Though faced with these circumstances, I refused to make excuses and kept driving forward with my personal, educational, and career goals. You already read that I have seven degrees, an accomplishment that I, of course, am super proud of. Also, I had each of my children while I was in school, and my five graduate degrees (including an MBA and a Juris Doctor) were completed while raising my kids and working full-time in Fortune 50 senior leadership positions. Did I say I was crazy? And if you are wondering, yes, I do manage to sleep!

One thing I've learned on my journey is that when life pushed back on me with its challenges, I used the lessons it taught me to tackle adversity and press forward. I learned not to let others' expectations define me and determine my capabilities. I worked through new and unfamiliar circumstances, pursued my goals, and left the naysayers on the sidelines.

In my corporate career, I worked on many multi-billion-dollar programs that have helped to keep the United States military the best in the world. Additionally, I have been involved in projects that have improved quality of life and increased life expectancy. While serving as a Judge Advocate in the Army National Guard, I got to be a part of a team that was mobilized to help navigate the early stages of the COVID pandemic. I've also been overseas training the Armed Forces of Liberia legal team. Personally, I'm a third-degree black belt in Tae Kwon Do, active in many community service projects, sit on a number of boards, and an executive partner at the University of Southern California Masters of Business for Veterans (MBV) program. I'm very fortunate to be in good health and most importantly, I'm happy.

Now ask yourself … are you happy with your career? What about your personal life? Do you feel like something is missing?

If so, it's time for you to make a change, and you already know this. Guess what? You've picked up this book and I'm here to help you and to challenge you on your journey.

This book will use powerful examples to help you make the decisions needed to succeed. By providing insights and analogies to the personal side of life and offering a perspective on choices we make in our careers, this book will show you how you can suit up and show up to life to live the life that you want. It will challenge you to find your identity and your vision. This book will also help you define and accomplish your life's ambitions. The focus is on *you* and what you want in life—no one else's expectations matter.

Together we will get you across your goal line. Be prepared to step onto the turf and explore past the boundaries of your comfort zone and the familiar. If you want to change your life and see different outcomes, it starts with you playing your game differently. Make today that day.

Remember that your past doesn't define you, though it has shaped you into who you are now and prepared you for what you want to become tomorrow. Winning in life is not about how you start; it's about how you finish. It's not about how slow or how fast you go, as long as you keep going. It's not about how other people define you; it's about how you want to define yourself.

What I want for you is to be the person who wakes up each day with purpose and intent, fueled by passion and determination. Be the one who refuses to be a spectator in life and always shows up ready to "play your game;" the person who is committed to never giving up. Be the player who believes anything is possible, and no matter what life throws your way, you have trained yourself to say, "I've got this!" Lastly, inspire others by showing them you moved the ball and found your greatness. Because success is not only measured by what you accomplish in life but also by what you inspire others to do.

By the end of this book, I hope my story, as well as the stories of the other great athletes and elite leaders in life that I've shared, leave you motivated to go after whatever it is you want in life.

The thing about time is that all of us have the same amount each day, no more, no less. Time is free, but it's priceless. You can't own it, but you can use it. You can't keep it, but you can spend it. Once it's spent, you can never get it back.

This chapter started off discussing how time flies. That's the bad news. The good news is you're the pilot. The winners in life use their time wisely to fly in the direction they want to go, and they make those 86,400 seconds each day count. All the others squander it away daily.

There are two types of people in life: *those who believe they can do anything* and *those who believe they can't.* Both are right. Which one do you want to be? Since you're reading this book, I'm going to go out on a limb and say the former. If that's the case, what really matters now is how you suit up, how you show up, and whether you move the ball. This book will help you to do that. Are you ready? Let's go. It's time to get off the sideline and back in the game.

CHAPTER 2:
TOMORROW IS NEVER PROMISED

"Passion is what makes life interesting, what ignites our soul, fuels our love and carries our friendships, stimulates our intellect, and pushes our limits."
—*Pat Tillman*

There isn't much in life that is certain. Well, let's see, there's death, taxes, oh yeah, one more thing: *life will not always go as planned.* Can I get an amen to that one?

I mean, think about that for a minute. How many times have you set a plan in motion only for it to get derailed and not go how you envisioned? Ah yes, that's all a part of the twists and turns we experience on this curvy road called life.

If there's one thing living through the COVID pandemic has taught us, it's that life can be extremely uncertain, and you never know what tomorrow may bring. It also served as another reminder that *tomorrow is never guaranteed* (I'll get back to this part shortly).

Going back to the first point, the plan we have for ourselves sometimes just gets thrown completely out the window due to circumstances out of our control or things we never could've foreseen. Pandemic, or for some other reason. Yep, it happens, you know it does. Go ahead, nod your head.

I want to run it back and share a part of my story from before the pandemic.

Throughout my life, when it came to my career, I always prided myself on being someone who had a plan. I set SMART goals, I knew what I wanted to be when I grew up, and I put together a roadmap for how I could achieve it. Little did I know that *one* phone call would completely change all of that and turn my world upside down. I'll get to this in a minute.

First, let's discuss my original plan. My big, long-term career goal was to be a Fortune 500 CEO. Pretty ambitious, right?

While it was a lofty goal, this wasn't something out of reach for me. I had been blessed with opportunities to excel and climb the corporate ladder in my twenties, landing a senior management job with a Fortune 50 company, The Boeing Company. My peers were in their forties and fifties, yet there I was excelling in a male-dominated field.

I was labeled as one of those "high potential employees" or "hi-pots." I earned a reputation for being a quick study and someone who you could put in charge of challenging projects that could get the job done.

One thing I picked up on early in my career was that I needed to think of myself as the "quarterback" of the game, driving how I would advance instead of merely relying on others to promote me. With that in mind, I was always looking for ways to differentiate myself from others and concentrated on building up great bullet points for my resume. I focused on networking and being visible to senior executives. Additionally, I made sure to link up with some accomplished mentors, including one who later went on to becoming the CEO of Boeing.

Life seemed to be good. I continued to ascend the corporate ladder and I kept crushing it on my performance reviews. I switched employers to take an amazing role within General Electric's Aviation division and continued to advance my career. The bullets on the resume got more and more impressive. I knew I was positioning myself on the path to one day achieve that CEO goal.

That's what I thought, at least. Now let's get back to that phone call that changed everything.

On the early evening of November 28, 2016, I was in Grand Rapids, Michigan, sitting in my dining room when my cell phone rang. I grabbed my iPhone and saw it was my mom calling. Instead of answering the phone, I said, "I'm too busy. I'll call her back later."

You see, I talked to my mom multiple times a week and didn't think there was anything unusual about why she was calling. But this time, it was different. Her purpose for the call was to let me know that my dad had passed away.

My dad had not been sick and there had been no warning signs or indication that he was going to leave us soon. His death was completely unexpected.

So, what happened? That morning, my dad told my mom that he was feeling great. He did however experience chronic pain and took pain medication that often made him drowsy. He told my mom he was going to take a nap in the living room. An hour later, my mom was cooking in the kitchen and my dad's cell phone rang. He didn't answer. My mom then checked his phone. She tried to wake up my dad, but it was too late. He had already passed. It was that quick. No warning, nothing. The lesson: *tomorrow is never promised to anyone.*

It always bothered me that I didn't answer my mom's phone call because I said I was "too busy." While taking the call would not have changed the outcome, it made me think about *what the hell am I too busy doing?*

My goal was to get to the C-suite in a Fortune 500 company, so I was busy being a jet setter and a workaholic. There were times I would come home with one suitcase only to grab another suitcase that was already packed by the door to go on another trip the next day. I was working my ass off trying to create a resume that was even more remarkable and that would help me achieve that dream.

After my dad passed away, I did a lot of reflecting and realized two things:

1. *You really are replaceable in the corporate world, and*

2. *When you go, the world keeps moving whether you're in it or not.*

I'd heard people talk about being replaceable before, but quite honestly, I never thought that applied to me. Was I naïve? Yes.

Because I had been advancing in my career and had these stellar performance reviews, I thought, "Well, if I were to leave the company, it would be a huge gap. They would surely miss me." What I realized during my reflection was that while some people might miss me, the business wouldn't just stop because I was gone. They would find a replacement, and while that new person might not be as smart or talented, the company would figure it out and keep on operating in my absence.

I also came to the realization that when my time was up on this Earth, the world would also keep moving forward without me; that impressive resume I'd been building would've been long forgotten. I mean, who would care about any of these bullets I had on that piece of paper? No one else but me. The seven college degrees, the billion dollar deals I used to work on, none of that would matter. What people would remember though was the legacy that I could leave behind.

So, I thought to myself, what would that legacy be? Three years before my dad's passing, I had published my *Move the Ball* book. After that book was published, I was given many opportunities to speak in the corporate setting on my Move the Ball philosophies and methodologies. But I really wanted to make an impact in the sports community.

When *Move the Ball* was published, do you think anyone from professional or college football was calling me wanting to know more about what I had to say or to invite me to speak to their organization? Nope. Not one single phone call.

When I tried to reach out and network with people from the sports industry, none of them were excited about what I, as a woman, who didn't grow up in a football family or have a dad who was a legendary coach or any sports connections, could share with them. People told me I was wasting my time. They said things like "none of these players care about what you have to say."

While I was disappointed by these types of responses, I wasn't devastated. I understood that not everyone was going to see my worth or align with my vision. This lesson holds true for all of us with anything in life. But here's the thing to keep in mind: *when someone doesn't believe in you, realize that their understanding or affirmation is not necessary for your progress.*

When people give you a negative response or a door essentially closes, you then have a choice to make—ignore their opinion and keep going or let them deter you from what you set out to do. I chose to do the former and kept putting out content in the world and influencing people on how they could "move the ball" and go after the life they wanted. The chapter titled "With or Without You" will expand on this and how to better deal with rejection.

So, what did I do? I took control of the life I wanted to live. I showed up every day, being consistent with my messages and my actions. That's when the magic happened and a transformation occurred. In the beginning, I thought *Move the Ball* was just going to be a book about football. Yes, I booked speaking gigs and held corporate workshops to teach and train on my leadership methods, but that is as far as I thought it would go.

Over time though, the Move the Ball brand evolved from a book about football to becoming a movement about how the competitive athlete mentality could help you move forward in life. It was broader than just football. The Move the Ball movement represented hope and never giving up. It was about how your past didn't define you or where you could go in life. It was about taking ownership, showing up in every single moment like you were supposed to be there, dominating the game, and going after the life that you wanted and that you deserved.

Years ago, people started posting on social media or writing to me sharing their accomplishments and how they had "moved the ball." They also started using *#movetheball* in their posts, back when hashtags were a newer thing. It was then that I realized that Move the Ball had become a way of life for people. I knew this was the legacy that I was meant to leave behind. That Fortune 500 CEO job that I had spent over a decade working towards no longer mattered. It's funny how life changes things on you.

I believe sometimes our lives need to be completely shaken up and totally rearranged for us to be placed in the position where we are truly meant to be. I never thought that I would be doing anything but working in a corporate environment. I loved it and I had been thriving in it.

When my dad passed away, that all changed. I realized my true purpose was influencing others through my Move the Ball movement. I told myself that one day I would quit my corporate job to focus on growing the movement and making a larger impact. After all, this was my legacy, so I would go all in and leave my mark on the world.

Being a single parent with five kids, I couldn't do the super bold thing and quit my job right away. No, I wasn't going to set myself up for failure. I spent some time planning out the business aspects and started networking with super successful entrepreneurs. While I was a lawyer, had an MBA, and had worked in multiple Fortune

50 companies, I had never run my own business and wanted to learn from those who had been out there crushing it. Preparation is important in anything you do in life, right? We will talk more about this in the "Suit Up" chapter.

Making the leap from corporate was also a very difficult thing to do. While I was emotionally ready to go, from a practical standpoint, leaving my guaranteed income source wasn't easy. I had a good paying job and I was also the primary breadwinner for my family. So, you see how this complicated things. After pushing back my leave date a couple of times, I finally decided to do it. On November 5, 2019, which would have been my dad's birthday, I hung up my corporate cleats and went all in on growing the Move the Ball movement, never looking back.

I had a plan and was ready to execute it. But remember that third certainty I mentioned earlier? Life won't always go as planned, and that is what happened yet again. In March 2020, the world changed drastically and shut down because of the Coronavirus pandemic.

People asked me how my business was going and commented, "Wow Jen, this is really bad timing for you."

My response was "No, this isn't bad timing. This is just one more thing that I have to figure out and I'm going to have a great story on the other side of it."

Remember what I said about choices? Well, I had a choice: *let fear of the unknown and this pandemic stop me or keep moving forward.* Of course, I chose the latter.

Every day, I suited up with a positive mindset and was ready to take on the day. I showed up every single day, focusing on the things I needed to so I could continue to grow the movement and the brand. I didn't back down and aggressively pushed forward. I was determined to move the ball and be a leader out there, positively influencing others.

I also kicked off the *Move the Ball* podcast on February 3, 2020. The show released two episodes each week featuring conversations with professional athletes and successful entrepreneurs on how the competitive athlete mentality could help people succeed in business, branding, and sports. The Move the Ball movement continued to grow in popularity. Remember how I mentioned those people in sports who weren't interested in what I had to say way back when? That all changed.

When I focused on growing the Move the Ball brand full-time, it was crazy to see the number of professional athletes who gravitated towards and stood behind the movement. Football players who have won multiple Super Bowls and college football national championships have seen the value of what it stands for. The impact that this movement has made on the world was more than I originally envisioned. My life didn't go according to my plan (remember, I said that's a certainty). Still, I knew that when I embarked on the journey, I had truly stepped into my purpose, and God had taken my greatest pain and turned it into my greatest calling.

Now here's the lesson for you. Tomorrow is promised to none of us. Therefore, it's important that we figure out what our "why" in life is, focus on our passion, and live each day intentionally and in a manner that aligns with that vision. Once we have that clarity, it's all about taking decisive action. People who walk with purpose don't need to chase people or opportunities. Their light causes people and opportunities to pursue them. It's never too late to start something new, reinvent yourself, or change your destination. Stop letting fear paralyze you and step into who you were meant to be. There's no better time like the present to do that. Afterall, your days are never guaranteed.

Think back to when you were a kid. Back then you had dreams of what you would become when you grew up. No matter how old we are, we all dream and aspire to be great individuals and have stellar accomplishments. We have visions of what we would like to do with our lives. Of course, that may change over time, too. A sad truth though is that most people never turn their childhood dreams into reality. Why not?

The biggest reason is fear—the apprehension to venture into that unfamiliar and uncomfortable zone. Everyone faces uncertainty and ambiguity. It's part of life's game. Great players learn to cope with change. The others shy away from or resist it.

I realize there are other reasons and we all have different thoughts for not pursing one goal or another. While some of them may be legit, those explanations are only valid for a length of time. There are other times when we are simply making excuses. If you want to be successful, you must hold yourself accountable. Focus on the objective and follow through on your action plans. You can do it. I know you can. The first step is breaking through the comfortable *I-will-do-it-later* mentality.

Reflect on the tough challenges you have overcome. Pat yourself on the back. You should be proud of your accomplishments. You have grown over the years. But as you sit at your office desk or in your seat in the classroom, what do you daydream about? Is it about what you want in life? Don't be stuck in a dream. I wrote this book because I want to help you turn those visions into reality. Life's too short to not live it in a way that you find fulfillment and joy.

I'm a firm believer that your life is no place to dream small. If others hadn't dreamt big, we would not have televisions, iPads, smartphones, GPS navigation systems, Facebook (excuse me, now called Meta), and Skype, to name a few. Each of these inventions and ideas started off as someone's daydream. We have these things today because these individuals didn't leave it to just a thought. They possessed the drive to execute and make these dreams happen.

When Orville and Wilbur Wright were teenagers, they dreamt of taking flight—a feat never successfully done before. Many discounted the idea of airplanes taking to the skies. Not these young men. Determined to experience the power of flight, the Wright brothers were not going to let this dream go unfulfilled.

One thing you likely didn't know about these two guys is they were not scholarly students with high academic achievements under their belts. In fact, they were quite the opposite. The Wright brothers were mischievous boys who never graduated from high school. Yet they still had a dream and were committed to seeing it through.

These siblings spent hours reading about aviation and aeronautics and learning from experiments of other flight inventors. One such inventor named Otto Lilienthal was unexpectedly killed in a glider accident in 1890. Wilbur spent days understanding Lilienthal's designs in order to further his knowledge of flight principles.

Orville and Wilbur spent the next thirteen years pursuing their dream. Yes, thirteen years. Then on December 17, 1903, over the sands of the North Carolina coast, their dream became a reality. Orville Wright piloted the first powered airplane twenty feet off the ground. His flight lasted twelve seconds and he traveled one-hundred and twenty feet. They made three more flights that day with Wilbur piloting the record flight of fifty-nine seconds and traveling eight hundred fifty-two feet.

They had done it! The Wright brothers started off their journey as two bicycle mechanics with a dream. They finished by making history. Orville and Wilbur were the fathers of flight. Can you imagine what today would be like if we didn't have airplanes as a mode of transportation? On any given day in the United States alone, greater than 45,000 flights take to the skies with almost three million airline passengers and flying more than 29 million square miles of airspace. This flight thing started because of these two men and their dream.

Ok, I get it. You might not think your dreams are on the same scale as the Wright brothers. Then let's take Landau Eugene Murphy Jr. as an example. In November 2010, Murphy and his wife left their home in West Virginia and headed to New York City where they stood for over twelve hours, among thousands of other performers, waiting to audition for the sixth season of NBC's hit reality television show, *America's Got Talent.*

Murphy's dream was to be a professional singer. So, there he stood, waiting for what could be a life-changing opportunity. He left his car washing job behind and decided to take a chance in life. Murphy didn't come from a family of fortune and wealth. His father was a coal miner and his parents divorced when he was eight years old. He then lived with his mom and four siblings in Detroit, Michigan. Life was hard-hitting for Murphy and he dropped out of school in the eleventh grade to support his family. Challenges continued and Murphy wound up homeless as a teenager. Shortly before heading to the show, he was robbed of all of his belongings. As he stood in front of the judges on the New York City stage, he wore the only jacket and pants he owned.

I watched the show when Murphy took the stage. His appearance was deceiving. I certainly did not expect this disheveled looking man to put on much of a performance (shame on me for having that initial impression). When the music started playing and Murphy began to sing, my jaw dropped in amazement. Wow, what a unique singing style.

On another television show, *The Voice,* the contestants initially perform on stage in the beginning of the season, while the judges are facing away from them just listening to musical talent without the consideration of physical appearance. If Murphy had been on that show, the judges would have thought it was Frank Sinatra up there on stage. When Murphy started singing, he sounded just like Sinatra, it was mesmerizing. The *America's Got Talent* judges agreed and gave him an outstanding ovation when he was done. Murphy also won the hearts of Americans from coast to coast.

On September 14, 2011, this young man was named the winner of *America's Got Talent*. There he stood on the stage—victorious. Murphy had done it, all because he had the courage to follow his dream. Since the show, Murphy has released four albums. Let this story inspire you.

In life, the possibilities are endless. You are no different than the Wright brothers and Landau Eugene Murphy Jr. You are capable of achieving anything you want in life. Commit to making it happen and don't be afraid to take risks. Take a chance and you'll be surprised at the outcome.

Ever since I was a kid, I loved the game of American football. It armed me with the principles I need to succeed on and off the football field. While falling in love with the game, I learned about how the outcomes were uncertain. You can't predict what will happen in a football game. Every Sunday during the NFL football season, and every Saturday in college football, this principle is proven to be true. Similarly, you can't forecast what will occur in your life. There is no crystal ball.

Every day, you make choices that will or will not get you closer to achieving your goals. It doesn't matter if you feel like you are the "underdog," or are the person with a perceived advantage, playing the game of life. As the quarterback on your field, you must take ownership of the game and drive the ball movement. You cannot always control what happens in life, though you can control how you respond. In this book, I share numerous football examples that prove just how uncertain a game can be.

Remember that some people go through life without ever showing up to play the game. They don't make the commitment to achieve greatness and therefore don't realize their dreams. Winning starts from within. You have one life and you deserve to be happy. Make the pledge today to start moving forward.

As I've already mentioned, don't let anyone else's expectations define who you should be. No matter who you are, you can be what you dream of becoming; you can be as great as you imagine. My story is proof of that. People told me I had no business being in football, and yet I have had the opportunity to sit on the board of, and be a consultant to, multiple semi-pro and pro football organizations, as well as coach professional athletes, entrepreneurs, and corporate executives on how to position their brands to attract the opportunities they want and drive revenue growth. I get to help them to move the ball.

What's the magic formula? Well first you have to commit to transforming your ideas from paper to actuality. Once you identify your goals, you need to focus on making it happen. This might mean coming up with a different approach. That's not shocking. As human beings, we tend to plan within the walls of what's comfortable and familiar. It's time now to break that habit. Again, the principles in this book will help you to do just that.

Never forget that you've got one life to live. Tomorrow is never promised. Now that I've shared a part of my story as well as a few other examples, make the decision to get out there and live in your purpose.

COACH'S CHALKBOARD

1. Your life is no place to dream small—dream big.

2. Make sure you're chasing purpose, not paper.

3. All great things started out as somebody's daydream.

4. It's your life, go after what ignites your soul. Don't be a spectator.

5. No one has the power to shatter your dreams unless you give it to them.

6. Live with purpose, passion, and intention today.

7. Tomorrow is never promised to anyone.

CHAPTER 3:
WHAT COLOR IS YOUR JERSEY?

"Champions are made from something they have deep inside
them – a desire, a dream, a vision."
—Muhammad Ali

The team uniform. While many young athletes take the meaning of the uniform for granted, that jersey they suit up with for practice or for gameday has meaning, more so than just being an article of clothing guaranteed to get dirty. That uniform represents unity, equality, and importantly, a team's identity.

As players in the game of life, we also need to be clear on our own personal identity. Too often, people struggle with having clarity of purpose and consequently end up feeling like they are just going through the motions of the day-to-day. What results is feeling a sense of emptiness and they quite often go to bed feeling unfulfilled. Does this sound familiar at all?

If you want to live a satisfying and exciting life, an important first step is getting clear on exactly what color the "jersey" is that you are wearing. In other words, who are you and what game are you playing? Without this clarity, it's difficult and pretty much impossible to have meaningful goals, you know, those goals that really excite your soul. Without these goals, you don't have real growth or significant change in life. It all ties together: *clarity, goals, growth, and change.*

A common theme in my social media posts, digital content, and speaking engagements centers on how realizing your dreams starts with YOU, no one else. So, you must take a hard look at yourself in the mirror and assess what you really want in life. Are you clear on your assignment (meaning your role and your purpose) and secondly, are your actions in alignment with that assignment? This is a topic that retired NFL player, Alex Molden, and I discussed on Season 2 of my Move the Ball podcast regarding his journey from being a 1st round NFL Draft pick and playing eight seasons in the NFL to his transition out of the League and becoming a successful speaker and coach.

In the sport of American football, as an example, the near-term objectives are simple—win football games. Each player on the team knows what jersey they are wearing, what their assignment is, and their actions are usually in alignment with that assignment. When the game clock expires, if that team has more points on the scoreboard than their opponent, they have achieved their objective and won the game. Through this chapter, our focus is going to be on understanding your assignment and your goals.

Simon Sinek, author of the book *Find Your Why: A Practical Guide for Finding Purpose for You and Your Team*, wrote that it's only when you understand your "why" (or your purpose) that you'll be more capable of pursuing the things that give you fulfillment. It will serve as your point of reference for all your actions and decisions from this moment on, allowing you to measure your progress and know when you have met your goals.

In life, we can agree that the journey down the field is irrelevant if you do not know which direction you are headed. When you suit up, you need to know what jersey you are putting on and what wearing that jersey means. Gaining this clarity is essential if you want to be a high performer in life or an elite athlete in sports. Both groups are clear on their intentions, and they suit up and show up each day in a consistent way.

Knowing your "why" provides clarity in your life. People who have a sense of purpose are often seen as relentless and unstoppable. They are laser-focused on their goals and shape their lives in the ways they want. They do not question their assignment and are clear on what they need to accomplish each day. On the other hand, those who do not know their purpose aren't clear on what they want out of life and are prone to wasting time and simply existing and floating through life, settling for whatever comes their way. This also can lead to confusion and can cause people to lose confidence.

Knowing your why also infuses you with passion for your goals. When you know your purpose in life, you are more deeply committed to pursuing things that matter to you. The idea behind this is that you'll never have to settle for less than what you want in life. When you have this clarity of purpose, it's easier to avoid distractions, keep your mind on your mission, stay in position, and achieve your vision.

Oh, by the way, numerous studies have shown that having a purpose in life leads to longer lifespans in older adults. This may be because when you are living with a purpose, you adopt a prospective focus, looking forward to the day when your purpose is fulfilled. This causes everyday stressors to become less influential and have a smaller impact on your overall well-being.

People who have a deeper sense of purpose in life are more resilient. They are better at understanding setbacks and unpleasant situations compared to those who wander through life aimlessly. When you know your purpose, you have a feeling of mastery that helps you let go of anything that goes wrong in your life that is irrelevant to your core values. This means you can learn from life's hardships and bounce back quickly from adversity.

Those who know their purpose live with integrity and understand who they are and what they are here for. They are more satisfied in general because they're living true to their core values. When this is the case, a person doesn't have to put on a façade or act like they are passionate about a job that they truly dislike. Instead, their passion is genuine for everything they do, and they always show up as their true selves.

If you aren't familiar with the name Brendon Burchard, Brendon is a *New York Times* best-selling author, globally respected high-performance coach, and according to *O, the Oprah Magazine,* "one of the most influential leaders in personal growth." Success Magazine also ranked Brendon in the Top 25 Most Influential Success Teachers along with Oprah Winfrey, Dr. Phil, Tony Robbins, Tim Ferriss, Arianna Huffington, and Deepak Chopra. In Brendon's book, *High-Performance Habits (How Extraordinary People Become That Way),* he lists developing clarity as the #1 habit of highly effective leaders, and he suggests four areas that form the basis of building long lasting and high performance:

1. **Self**: Get very clear on who you are and what you want in this stage of life.

2. **Social**: Have clear intentions about how you want to treat other people. Develop high situational awareness and social intelligence.

3. **Skills**: Be clear on the skills you need to develop and obsessively build upon those skills.

4. **Service**: Consider your contribution to the world. Are you engaged in meaningful and fulfilling service to others?

By examining these four areas, you are embarking on a journey of self-awareness, and Brendon's book goes into greater detail for each of these areas. By "knowing yourself", you can better connect with the future path that you desire and gain a better understanding of your contribution to the world. Think about how you can add value to the people around you this week. Or is there someone in your life who needs your help? Figuring out how you can best serve others is one great way to gain clarity around your purpose and your identity. But wait there's more. We need to further unpack the "understanding who you are" piece of this.

When football players leave the locker room to head out onto the field, they're suited up with their helmet, uniform, pads, and cleats. They're also clear about what team they're on and their team's objectives. Now you need to look within yourself and recognize what your core values are. Understanding who you are and what you stand for is a defining moment. This is not a check-the-box type of exercise and you should spend quite a bit of time answering this question. It is a critical one.

Let's start by answering this question: *What does it mean to seek clarity?*

This means remaining focused on today, here in the present moment, while thinking about tomorrow and the future. It means thinking through the following questions:

- *Who are you?*
- *What is it about you that makes you special?*
- *What is it that you want out of life?*
- *What do you find meaningful and fulfilling?*
- *What things do you do that makes other people's lives better?*
- *What activities are fun for you?*
- *What did you like doing as a kid?*
- *What do people ask of you when they come to you for help?*
- *What specific talents do you have?*

- *If you learned you only had one more year to live, what would you be doing?*

- *What kinds of things are you willing to go the extra mile for?*

- *If given the chance to teach others, what would you teach them?*

- *If you were given the chance to do something you love and not have to worry about the paycheck, what would that be?*

While these seem like pretty basic questions and things to know, you might be surprised that very few people have thought about them and taken time to figure out the answers. These are questions you should be thinking through today as they will help lay the foundation for your future going forward.

When seeking clarity and trying to discover yourself, it's also important to distinguish values from ethics and morals. While all three provide behavioral rules, each of these concepts has different meanings. Morals define a person's character, whereas ethics stress a social system where standards or codes of behavior are expected by a group to which an individual belongs. Examples are professional ethics and company ethics. Therefore, while a person's moral code remains relatively unchanged over time, the ethics one practices can be dependent on others. Morals can have a social element to them, but they are far more about good and bad than other elements. Society thus judges more strongly on morals than values.

Now let's discuss values, which we will spend a little bit more time on. Values are different from ethics and morals because they encompass our fundamental beliefs. They provide you with guidance on how you can live your best life. Below are some examples of values to get you thinking about which ones are most important to you. The two types of values identified are those that are career-focused and those that just apply to life in general.

Neither of these lists below are intended to be all-inclusive or representative of what might be the values that you hold important. Some of these may resonate with you, while others may not. These are just a few to get your brain thinking.

Now, to really understand what jersey you should be wearing and what game it is you should be playing, it's time for you to go through this two-step exercise.

Step #1: Make a list of values that fit into these categories.

First, answer the questions provided in the section above. Then grab a sheet of paper and make two columns of values where you will add to the ones provided in the columns below. Under career, other examples could include: being a team player, having power, and having time freedom. Under life, you might also list: fidelity, spirituality, and optimism. Several ideas have been provided for you. Now it's your turn. Keep adding to the lists.

VALUES – CAREER	VALUES – LIFE
Spending time with family and friends	Compassion
Advancing my career	Integrity
Taking risks	Respect for others
Having job security	Honor
Balancing work and home life	Courage
Having low work stress	Honesty
Being creative	Accountability
Having a high-paying job	Responsibility
Helping the community	Fairness
Being well-liked	Conformity
Collaborating with others	Encouragement

Step #2: Prioritize the values that are most important to you.

Next, review both lists of values. On another sheet of paper make two lists: one called "Life" and the other called "Career." For each of them, pick the five values you believe are the most important to you. This is what you think, not anyone else. Here, you get to put on the jersey that you want to wear. Forget about other's expectations when defining your core values. Identifying your top values should help you discover or become more aware of who you are at your core, and what really is important to you.

The reason you did this exercise is because the items you selected for your second list should always be factors when you are considering your purpose, your goals, and what you want out of life. It is important for you to be doing things that are in alignment with these values and don't require you to compromise them. It is worth noting that your values can, and likely will, change over time; there's nothing wrong with that. But it's always good to revisit these periodically to make sure that what you do in life is congruent with what's important to you.

Once you have clarity around your values and your core being, the next step is determining your goals. Realizing your dreams starts with YOU. Now that you have your jersey on and know what color it is, you need to focus on defining what game it is you want to play.

I know you know this, but having goals are important because without them, your journey through life will often be confusing, disappointing, frustrating, unrewarding, and a whole bunch of other negative stuff. Goals show us what we need to strive for. They determine what winning and what success looks like for us.

It's important to not only think about the big goals but remember the smaller ones as well. They don't all have to be BHAGs—big, harry, audacious goals. As dreamers in life, it's good for us to identify the larger ones, but little goals and smaller victories are not to be discounted or forgotten.

Whether they are bigger, stretch goals or ones that are more attainable in the shorter term, the important thing to remember is they need to be SMART goals.

S   =   Specific (I have sufficient detail.)

M   =   Measurable (I can measure it.)

A   =   Actionable (I can do something about it.)

R   =   Relevant (I am aligned with this goal.)

T   =   Time-bound (I have a set timeframe.)

Examples of SMART goals would be 1) I want to lose twenty-five pounds in three months and 2) I want to complete my master's degree in business within the next three years.

Throughout this book, I will continue to stress that life involves many choices. Here, you get to choose what you want your goals to be. What is the game you are playing and what does winning look like to you? You should define the game however you desire. That is up to you to decide.

What is it that you want for yourself? What are your dreams and your ambitions? Write them down. Think about all aspects of life—career, relationships, health, family, financial, and more. Be sure to include goals that address all three-time horizons too: short-term (1–2 years), medium-term (3–5 years), and long-term (5+ years). Reach far and set high expectations for yourself. Remember your past does not define you, and you can go after anything you want moving forward. Do not let your past circumstances limit your vision for the future. Now is the time to identify those goals that energize your spirit and ignite your passion. Once you have that figured out, then you can put your playbook together and really go after them. That is when you can really focus and ensure that your actions are in alignment with your assignment.

I hope that from reading this chapter, the wheels are turning in your mind and if you haven't done so already, you spend some time mapping out what it is you really want in life and write down those goals. Then put them somewhere that you can see them as a continual reminder that this is what you are after.

Once you have finished reading this book, it's my hope that your life changes drastically. That is up to you, of course. It's going to depend on what you choose to do differently after getting through the rest of these chapters. How will you suit up and show up each day to move the ball? That's going to be key. Knowing what jersey you're wearing and what game you are playing is just the beginning. The strategies, tools, principles, and stories shared throughout this book will get you fired up so you can turn your goals into actuality.

COACH'S CHALKBOARD

1. Get clear on your purpose and what you want to do in life.

2. Without clarity, it's hard to develop meaningful goals.

3. Define who you are before you play the game.

4. Never let anyone discourage you from your ambition for a better life.

5. Determine what "winning" means to you.

6. Set SMART goals.

CHAPTER 4:
OWN YOUR GAME

"Your mind is what makes everything else work."
—Kareem Abdul-Jabbar

In sports and in life, how you show up to the game matters. Unfortunately, most people get this part all wrong. They never fully "show up" ready to play, and consequently, they never truly reach greatness. They simply exist, floating through life, and wondering why they ended up where they did and why they didn't accomplish more for themselves. Some people never cared. They have come to settle for what life throws at them and end up living a life that is unfulfilling or unrewarding.

You differ from these individuals because I know you really want to win. How do I know this? Because you chose to read this book which is about showing up the right way to get what you want out of life. So now, it's time to get in the game.

In life there are no guarantees. Most of us would like some sort of assurances before we commit to extraordinary goals. Wouldn't it be great if you knew that an outcome would work out in your favor before you even started? If only life were that easy. Then you wouldn't have to question decisions, take risks, or make the hard sacrifices. Unfortunately, the scenario with guarantees only happens in fairy tales. In the real world, there is no magical mirror, crystal ball, or psychic that can reveal your future.

Reality contains shades of gray (i.e. uncertainty) and is very unpredictable. Therefore, you must trust your feelings and your faith to guide you in the right direction. Your confidence will drive you to make choices that will get you closer to your goal. When you are focused, momentum will then take over. Before you know it, you will have won your game. It's important to remember that your success will not occur overnight but committing to the journey and trusting the process will take you where you need to go.

If you really want to achieve great things in life and be legendary, start with taking ownership. This means owning what game you are playing and then owning every single action, inaction, and outcome that occurs along the way to your success. The Coach's Corner will help you understand what this concept of ownership entails, and get you started suiting up to play your game the right way.

COACH'S CORNER

1. Own your game (Ownership)

2. Be 100% all-in (Commitment)

3. Trust yourself (Confidence)

4. Make hating to lose a priority (Accountability)

Step 1: Take complete ownership over the game.

In "What Color Is Your Jersey," you went through the process of gaining clarity and centering on what was important to you in life. Through a period of reflection, you identified your core values and determined what your goals are across several different categories, including business and career.

Taking ownership over your life requires you to be like a postage stamp. Meaning you need to stick with your journey until you reach your destination. No matter where the path may take you, it's about staying the course as you go through the hills and the valleys.

You will not attract what you want in life and achieve the outcomes you seek until your *commitment*, your *attitude*, and your *actions* reflect the desired outcome. That starts with taking ownership over your life and what you want. To "own your game," you need to be 100% committed to your goals. Don't say it's what you want if you aren't completely ready to play the game and own the journey.

Ownership means not playing the victim when things don't go your way. Ownership means suiting up and bringing the best version of yourself forward each day. Ownership means showing up to play the game even on the days that you don't feel like it. Ownership means that no matter what you are going through, you are going to give it your all, try your best, and when things don't work out the way you want, you are going to pick yourself back up and figure out how to continue to move forward.

All of that is what it means to own your game. So now, look at the goals you have identified for yourself. How badly do you want them? Are you willing to make the sacrifices and trade-offs required to pursue them? If you aren't ready or willing to alter your behaviors and lifestyle to accomplish what you claim is important to you, then perhaps you need to re-evaluate what game you want to play. Don't rush through this process. Only you can determine what makes you happy, what you want, and how you will define success.

It's important that you repeat your goal-setting process until you are comfortable with the goals you have identified and are ready to take complete ownership over them. Once you have completed this, proceed to Step 2.

Step 2: Make the commitment to be in the game.

If you want to move the ball and win, you need to bring your A-game to the field. To do that, you must be committed on a mental, emotional, and physical level. It's time to be real. Check yourself. Are you working towards your goals or are you simply going through the motions? How are you suiting up and showing up? Are you *in the game* one day and *out of the game* the next?

Each day we make choices. Some of them are tougher than others. Easier choices might be what to wear or what to eat each day. Other decisions that require more deliberateness involve whether you will take a risk today, what tasks you will work on, and if you will stay focused on the right activities to get you closer to your goal line. These decisions tie to your commitment level and to your ownership.

When I was in the early stages of writing *Move the Ball*, I contemplated attending a small group writing seminar. But I was unsure. I teetered on whether I really wanted to go through all the trouble of getting to this writing workshop. First, I lived in Michigan at the time and the course was in Oklahoma. So, what was the big deal there? Well, not only would I need to take a week of vacation from work, but I would also need to buy an airplane ticket, pay for a hotel room, reserve a rental car, and more. Did I really want to do this and incur all these expenses? I was on the fence. For months I wobbled back and forth.

Then I thought about it some more. If I was serious about writing my book, then I needed to act like I was. I needed to commit, take ownership, and be all-in. While I only had a limited amount of accrued vacation, it was worth spending my hard-earned vacation on this seminar. Afterall, this was supposed to be an investment, right? Yes, it was. This was an investment into something that was a priority to me. So, I was willing to do whatever it took to make this goal happen.

First, I registered for the class. It was about eight weeks before the session. Then I made all my travel arrangements and went to Tulsa. The five days of the course went by quickly, but I learned so much. It was well worth the use of my time and money. The experience taught me a lot about how to be a better writer and about the industry. The best part was that I met incredible people who became a crucial part of my team going forward. I brought them into my huddle (I'll discuss the huddle later in this book) and they were instrumental in me publishing *Move the Ball* when I did. They kept me motivated, and I was showing up and playing the game.

Move the Ball is the thing that started the Move the Ball movement, which has since grown into so much more with the podcast and the various campaigns and ventures involving the brand. Without this book, I probably would not be on the path that I am on today, getting to work with very successful professional athletes and executives on their brands, business opportunities, and other incredible projects.

By taking ownership and being 100% committed to achieving my goal of publishing a book (about the parallels between football and life), it set my life in a different direction. During a business trip where I was doing a speaking event for a Fortune 100 client, my driver asked me how long it had taken me to write *Move the Ball*. I told him it took me about a year. He then said, "That year changed your life." He was right!

Years ago, I had the opportunity to hear Tom Bilyeu, serial entrepreneur and co-founder of Quest Nutrition, share his experience of starting a healthy protein bar and powder company, and the journey to its explosive growth. In 2010, Bilyeu co-founded Quest Nutrition with his friends Ron Penna and Mike Osborn. The company grew by 57,000% in its first three years and was ranked #2 on the Inc. 500 fastest growing companies in the United States in 2014. By the end of 2015, Quest products were being sold at over 40,000 points of distribution in over 70 countries. In August 2019, Simply Good Food agreed to buy Quest Nutrition for $1 Billion.

While Quest Nutrition is a success story, the company's journey was not without obstacles and challenges. In the beginning, Tom and his co-founders started by running their technology company during the day and testing new recipes at night. After a year of doing this, they came up with a winning protein bar recipe, only to discover that the low-sugar product they had created was un-manufacturable. As it turned out, manufacturers told them that packaged food becomes virtually impossible to create with off-the-shelf manufacturing equipment once the sugar is stripped from the products.

Contract manufacturers said, "It can't be done," and in order for it to be done, they would have to compromise on the product they wanted to produce for Quest Nutrition. This was something that the Quest founders were unwilling to do.

Tom shared that at that point, they had a decision to make. And the question he posed out to all of us who were listening to his story was that when you are going after what you want in life, you must ask yourself this: *What will it take to get you to where you want to go and what are you willing to do?*

What he was getting at was you must decide to what lengths and to what risks you are willing to undergo to make your dreams a reality. For Tom and his partners, instead of balking at such a major roadblock with contract manufacturers, the team decided the only solution was to self-manufacture their product and do the necessary research to make their product shelf stable.

As you can imagine, this was a very capital-intensive decision they were making, but they were unwilling to compromise their product formulas as they wanted to stay in alignment with the goal of their company: *providing healthy and nutritious products that helped to end metabolic disease while still tasting good.*

So, coming back to the question of what they were willing to do to achieve their goal, this would require them to purchase their own equipment. They were so committed that they were willing to take on that risk. So, the three of them ended up purchasing the equipment and embarked on what Bilyeu referred to as an "absurd journey."

While the road ahead was filled with bumps and obstacles, in the end, their commitment and decision to go all-in and self-manufacture their products worked out for them, and the rest is history. The takeaway: *Are you willing to do what is required to achieve your goals? When you are truly committed to achieving what you want, you make the sacrifices and take the risks needed.*

You see, unless you make the commitment that is required for you to win, what you have is only promises and hopes, but no plans and no results. Commitment unlocks doors from your imagination and allows for further clarity for your vision. Commitment is the glue that bonds you to your goals. Today, get your head in the game and say, "I'm all in." Be ready to take action and stick with the journey no matter how bad the road ahead may be. Those who remain committed transform their goals from ideas to actuality.

Step 3: Trust your decisions.

Throughout this book you will find the key to accomplishing your goals is making changes to the way you think and how you act. If you want to be a winner, you need to mentally prepare for change and transformation, and then you need to act accordingly.

This world is divided into two groups: people who are open to change and those who are closed to it. As I stated before, it's filled with people who think they can do anything and those who think they can't. The view you adopt for yourself affects every aspect of your life, from relationships to career moves to parenting decisions. Great leaders possess a desire to learn and challenge themselves to grow. They aren't afraid to change, and most importantly, they trust their decisions and what their gut has told them.

The players who are successful in life aren't afraid to take risks. They choose creativity over certainty, meaning they come up with non-traditional and innovative ways to take the shot at what they want in life instead of playing it safe. They get fired up over taking a half-court shot or a chance others won't take. They show up to win and they play to win.

Something guaranteed in life is that obstacles will come in our path and force us to find a new center of gravity and a new way to stand. It will make us pivot and deviate from our original plan, time and time again. We will have to make adjustments, just like teams do while playing football games, because the outcomes aren't going as planned.

While teams make shifts, they trust their decisions and they don't second guess why they are out there playing the game. They keep pushing forward. They understand that excuses will always be there but opportunities won't, so they can't back down. They continue to take ownership and show up in every single moment like they are supposed to be there. They believe in the decisions they have made and they keep progressing forward even when they don't have all the answers and they can't see the path ahead.

> " *I don't believe in looking back. If you make a decision that you think is the proper one at a time, then that's the correct decision."*
> —John Wooden, Legendary UCLA Basketball Head Coach

Your mindset frames the path you take in life. Not only is it important to have a positive outlook, but you also have to believe in yourself and possess a winning edge, knowing that the choices you make are the right ones. You are then going to take ownership over that and no matter what happens, you're going to remind yourself that the decisions you made were the correct choices at the time you made them. The next step will then be figuring out your subsequent moves and what your playbook needs to be from there. You don't need to know everything to get started, you just need to put together an initial plan, trust your decisions, and get moving. The next chapter, "Suit Up," will cover mindset and confidence in more detail.

Step 4: Start with a "Hate to Lose" Mentality & Hold Yourself Accountable

Accountability is that "A" word we hear about all the time. Great coaches, great leaders, and great players always mention how they hate to lose and how they will hold themselves accountable to the standard they have set for themselves. These individuals aren't just motivated to win, they do not like losing and are completely disciplined and dedicated to achieving their goals.

A question you need to ask yourself is: *Am I simply motivated or am I really dedicated to achieving my goals?*

There is a difference between these two. Many people look to motivation to push them toward their destination. But when that motivation wears off, then what? How do people stay committed on those days they don't feel like showing up and putting in the hard work? On those days where there are tasks that aren't sexy or fun and the ones that they really don't want to do?

The thing is that motivation will only get people so far, and when it reaches the end, there needs to be something else there to keep the kettle boiling. That "thing" is dedication. It's an integral part of the equation for success that many overlook.

One difference between motivation and dedication is *action*. Motivation involves the initiative required to start a task. It can include the desire to engage in a particular behavior or goal. But dedication goes beyond a mere desire. It ties to a person's commitment to following through with behaviors and actions. Dedication is the fuel that drives people to not want to lose.

Owning your game requires you to be disciplined, dedicated, and possess this hate-to-lose mentality. It also requires you to play to your standard and hold yourself accountable when you fall short of that standard. You won't get much done if you only hustle on the days that you feel good. Impossible dreams demand an impossible work ethic. You have to show up and put in the work that aligns with the standards you have set for yourself.

We know that no action means there will be no change in your life. Limited action will lead to limited change. But lots of purposeful action will lead to massive change and substantial changes in your life. Your grind may go unnoticed by others, but your results will not.

Having a hate-to-lose mentality means you show up every day and give it all you've got. It means you leave nothing in the tank and you do everything 110% so you feel good about how you performed each day. It's about devoting everything you have into your life and the game you are playing. This is what taking ownership truly entails.

Now that you have read this chapter on owning your game, you need to focus on a spectacular year ahead of you. Forget about any New Year's resolutions you have made and have since left behind. It's time for you to shine and get ready for a journey ahead with great accomplishments. Think about this: In a single year, you can completely reinvent yourself if you choose to show up every day and put in the work.

It starts with you taking *complete* ownership. It's time for you to jump in completely and go all in. When you throw yourself entirely into the game, you will be amazed at what you can achieve. It isn't going to be easy. If it was, then everyone would do it. Greatness doesn't happen overnight. There will be good days and bad days. Playing outside of your comfort zone can get ugly. You may question your decisions and your future. Relax. It's all part of the ride.

You have to let go of whatever is holding you back and make winning a priority, today. Forget your fears and the mistakes you have made. It's in the past. Leave it there. Now is the time for you to create your future.

In 1989, Jerry Jones bought the Dallas Cowboys football team from H.R. Bum Bright. Jones immediately fired successful and legendary head coach Tom Landry and hired Jimmy Johnson as the replacement. Landry had coached the Cowboys for twenty-nine years, leading the team to two Super Bowl championships in the 1970s. However, the last seasons of Landry's tenure had been losing ones. It was time for a change… in with Johnson, out with Landry. While the decision was a controversial one, sometimes change is needed. This doesn't take anything away from Landry's outstanding leadership and accomplishments, but Jones recognized he needed to switch it up.

> " *Do you want to be safe and good, or do you want to take a chance and be great?"*
> *—Jimmy Johnson*

Was it the right move? Some will say no. But let's look at the results that followed. During Johnson's coaching period, the Cowboys dominated in the NFL, winning consecutive Super Bowl titles. Johnson is only one of six coaches in professional American football history to achieve such a feat. Key to their success was the team's relentless attitude and their risk-taking on the field.

So, what does that mean for you? You have a decision to make. Do you want to stay inside your comfort zone and live your life as-is? Or do you want to take a chance and be great? You shouldn't be stuck in a daydream. It's time to bring all your great visions and aspirations to life.

You are either committed to mediocrity or you are committed to greatness. Which will it be? The decision is yours. If you choose the latter, then you must get in the game now and develop a serious attraction to winning. Remember, going after and achieving your dreams isn't about intelligence or natural-born talent. The concepts discussed here in this book will help you to get there. But ultimately, succeeding in life is up to you. You can have the career and the life you've always wanted. The tools and frameworks provided through this book will set you on the path to win. That's what you deserve.

So, get your game on, and trust that you will make the right decisions. I know you will. Now it's time for you to own your game, suit up, and be all in—never a little out.

COACH'S CHALKBOARD

1. You have a chance every single day to make a change and be the person you want to be.
2. A sense of ownership is one of the most powerful weapons you can have in life.
3. The road to success is through commitment.
4. Trust yourself—the game is mostly mental.
5. Always play to your standard.
6. Be married to the game.
7. Accept responsibility for your actions. Be accountable for your results.

CHAPTER 5:
SUIT UP

"Winning can be defined as the science of being totally prepared."
—George Allen

In sports, there are good athletes and there are great ones. In companies, there are good business people and there are exceptional ones. In life, business, and sports, there are good leaders and there are inspirational ones. No matter what the setting, factors exist that elevate the elite players and separate them from the rest. For them to be truly great, it starts with how these people suit up (what they do as part of their preparation) and then how they show up (what they do) to play their game.

To train like a great athlete, you must first be committed to winning. You must *want it* enough. The previous chapter stressed the importance of ownership, accountability, and personal commitment. To win in life, your inner spark must be charged and ready to detonate. Accomplished winners find the mental, physical, and emotional strength to persevere through adverse situations. That's what is necessary to reach those high levels of success.

In my *Move the Ball* book, I highlighted that elite players train for greatness by using the elements of MAD PRIDE to elevate their game. I explained each of the components of MAD PRIDE in extensive detail in *Move the Ball* and I will elaborate on many of these elements throughout this book too as they are critical to being able to suit up, show up, move the ball, and maneuver through the many twists and turns life might throw at you.

Everything begins with your mindset. Your thoughts, your attitude, and your determination are essential for success. This is all part of the "suiting up" process. You see, it's the choices you make in life that determine where you go. From what time you wake up, to what you eat, to how you dress, all those decisions that you make on a daily basis, and more, matter. They determine whether you are moving forward or moving backwards. It's just that simple.

When you've suited up with the right positive thoughts and the right mentality, it's easier to make choices that align with what you are trying to achieve.

But here's a twist. Decisions can also be turning points for us. They can be intimidating when you are navigating through uncertain situations or when you are really stretching yourself and pushing yourself out of your comfort zone to reach that next level of success.

Then the choices are not always that easy. There will be times you will question your vision and your plans. Doubt and fear of failure may deter you from progressing forward.

Additionally, we all have a voice inside us that tries to convince us that we cannot achieve our dreams. The strength of that voice usually is tied to our risk tolerance.

For some people, too, they have that voice that also tries to persuade them that they don't deserve to live the life they want. That could be because of some trauma or some abusive person in their life made that viewpoint known, which then led them to believe it themselves.

Whatever is driving that little dialogue, it's a conservative inner personality who wants you to remain in your safe zone. Your inner being is going to be cautious and will fill your mind with unpleasant and uncomfortable thoughts. It will come up with a hundred reasons why you shouldn't walk through the door of the unknown and why you should play life unadventurously.

"This is too difficult."

"I'm just not good enough at this, maybe I should forget about it."

"Somebody else is better than me, there's no sense in trying."

These are just a few examples of what your voice might be telling you. I could come up with 1,000 others.

The challenge for you is not to listen. Be stubborn. Push yourself out of that secure space and silence and calibrate your inner critic. That's part of suiting up—*nixing that internal doubt, believing in yourself, and being willing to bet on yourself.*

Throughout this book you will see several themes that I come back to, confidence and consistency being two of them. Suiting up requires you to be confident in your abilities to navigate through any environment, tackle any obstacle, and achieve any goal you set your mind to. I want to emphasize that having this confidence doesn't mean you know all the answers, have your plan perfectly laid out, or that you don't have any doubts going forward. Rather, confidence is telling yourself "No matter what, I know I can figure out what I need to learn, and what I need to do, to get me through this."

You see that's how high performers think. In their mind, they know that no matter what situation you throw them in, they know that they will figure something out and be just fine. That's what being confident is.

I think it's time for a quick football story. Joe Namath is known by football fans for many things, including being the New York Jets quarterback who took his underdog team to Super Bowl III and won in 1969. Leading up to that game, football commentators and fans speculated that the Baltimore Colts (today called the Indianapolis Colts) would win this match-up. Of course, Namath didn't let the hype phase him. Instead, he made sure he suited up the right way by spending hours mentally preparing for the game, reviewing game film, and practicing with his team. Namath had faith in himself, and his team, and they showed out on the field on game day. This boundless confidence translated to execution and the Jets ended up beating the Colts by a score of 16–7. The Jets were the Super Bowl III Champs. By trusting in himself and his abilities, this quarterback was able to lead his team to victory.

A friend of mine, Earl Christy, was on that team and hearing him re-tell the stories of winning that Super Bowl and what it was like for him to be on that team was pretty invigorating. That guy has a tremendous amount of energy for someone being in his seventies and you could just tell the conviction that he and that team had going into that championship game, determined to play their hearts out.

Now confidence is important. But suiting up is much more than that. The next piece really goes to your grit and determination. Dexter McCluster was an NFL running back who was drafted in the 2nd round of the 2010 NFL Draft by the Kansas City Chiefs. During his time both in college at Ole Miss and in the NFL, Dexter set a number of school, conference, and franchise records. One thing to mention about Dexter though is that he is only 5 foot 8 inches tall. Yep, Dex was a "little" guy (by NFL standards) but he was packed with power, speed, and explosiveness.

Something Dexter told me once when we talked about his success in football is that you have to be hungrier than the average person. "Every day you have to wake up in the morning, you have to walk in it, you have to talk it, and you have to really live it."

He continued to say,

> "If you really want something, you have to do the extra, whatever that extra is to you, you have to do it. Whether it's waking up at two o'clock in the morning, making that

sacrifice to do it. Working out, running, doing whatever, just put your mind to it. But when you say that, when you say you want something, you can't just say it and not mean it. So, when you say it, you have to believe it. Keep going. Be prepared to fall but be prepared to fight back because at the end of the day, nobody cares how you got there."

Dexter achieved his dream of playing in the NFL by always believing in himself, staying hungrier than most, and conditioning his mind to do whatever he needed to do each day to keep going. That's what you need to do as well.

Something I do every morning is I have sayings that I tell myself out loud to get me energized, fired up, and ready to dominate the day. It's called self-talk and it's part of how I suit up. I'm not going to tell you what you should be telling yourself in the mornings, but I would encourage you to create your own self-talk messages and use these to get yourself in the right place to take on the day. Calibrate what you say to yourself. It'll make a huge difference.

I would also encourage you to write a few notes to yourself so when the day isn't going your way, you can pull out those notes and they will reframe and reset you. In the back of this book, I have included a section called "Jen's Notes," where I share a few of the thoughts I wrote to myself at very vulnerable points in my life. I wanted to write down messages of positivity as a reminder to always keep me going. I'm sharing them with you in hopes that they will inspire you to write your own self talk messages of hope, encouragement, and to help keep you pushing forward, especially when times get rough.

Mental toughness is something that is talked about regularly when it comes to professional sports. Being an athlete at the highest level is taxing, both mentally and physically. Sure, there are perks and niceties of being a public figure, but there's a lot that goes with that too. Those that can't keep up their mental resiliency don't remain in the professional ranks for a long career. Being mentally strong is important "off the field" for us non-pro athletes as well.

Mental Toughness is one of those MAD PRIDE attributes that separates you from others playing the game. It gives you the edge over your competition. This toughness cannot only be psychological—rather, it's a combination of mental, physical, and emotional strength. These three aspects together will allow you to cope better than your opponents when faced with life's demands.

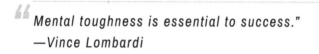

Mental toughness is essential to success."
—Vince Lombardi

Mental toughness means staying fixated on your goals and not being poorly affected by other people's pessimism. This focus requires blocking out what's not important. You must ignore any and all distractors and detractors. Block them out. They should not be in the field of play. We'll get into this more in another chapter that's called "With or Without You."

Mental toughness also requires you to condition your mind to remain confident, like I've already discussed. Mental toughness also means being tenacious and never giving in. It's about not letting anyone, or anything break you, no matter how ugly, difficult, frustrating, or demotivating your situation may get. You have to stay suited up, committed to moving that ball and reaching greatness. That is all on you. 90% of people give up on their dreams, inches from the finish line.

It's because they lack the mental stamina and mental discipline to continue to push and fight for what they want in life. Remember, anyone can give up. Learning how to hold it together when everyone else would understand if you fell apart, that's true strength. That's part of the mental game.

While suiting up is largely about the mental component, the positive mindset, the resiliency, and all of that, it doesn't stop there. What this is about is the preparation you need to be ready (mentally, physically, and emotionally) to show out and perform on those tasks you need to do each day. The "Keep Your Engine Tuned" chapter will go into quite a bit of depth on areas you should prioritize to help with this.

Another part of the suit up process entails your preparation and the morning routine that you have identified for yourself. Ask yourself what does your preparation look like today? Do you take time to map out what you should be doing on a weekly basis? If not, that's step one. You should have a clear picture of what it is you want to accomplish each week and what tasks are required to get there. Then you lay out what days you are going to devote to what activities. You've got to have a plan.

For me, Sundays are my big planning days for the week. I'm writing down my goals for the week ahead, I'm outlining my focus areas for each day, and I'm prioritizing my time accordingly. Then every day, as part of my morning "power hour" as I like to call it, I have carved out a part of that time to review my plan and also "time to think" which is some creative morning time to get my brain warmed up and ready to go for the day. Included in this preparation, I write down questions I want or need to get answers to so I can execute my plan for the day.

While for most people this kind of preparation isn't a fun activity, consequently they don't look forward to doing it. However, it's a necessity for being more efficient each day and maximizing your time in a productive manner. This also avoids the build-up of stress and anxiety as you have deadlines approach for various tasks. So, when you're suiting up, don't just get your mindset right, get your plan together too.

There's also a saying in sports, *always be ready so that you don't have to get ready.* That's also what this preparation is all about. Being ready to go at any moment because you've done the planning, the research, you've asked the right questions, you know what you need so when opportunities present themselves you don't have to get ready, you're already ready.

Here's one example of this in the professional setting. I speak quite often and train thousands on managing their personal brand. You should always have that "elevator speech" prepared because you never know who you're going to meet. In any setting, you want to be able to clearly articulate who you are and the value that you bring to the table. This isn't just if you're actively looking for a job, or funding for your business, or trying to grow your clientele. Opportunities are all about timing and the individuals in your network. So, when you come across people, you better be ready to openly communicate your brand to others.

Imagine you walk into an elevator and the CEO of your dream company is in there with you. You can't waste that opportunity. What is it that you would say to him or her? You need to have that canned spiel ready to go at any moment. That's part of always being ready. You don't want to fumble or drop the ball on that one because you didn't stay ready.

If you're playing to win in life, don't underestimate the power of suiting up. Now that's not the only thing that's going to get you across the goal line, of course you have to show up too, take action, and move the ball. But it's the mindset and the mentality you bring into each day that is going to largely define how your day ends.

As you are suiting up, don't focus on the struggles you might be facing, focus on the strength you have to overcome them. Always make sure you're including gratitude in your suit up process, that's one other element of my morning power hour. That positive attitude and one of appreciativeness will give you tremendous power over your circumstances instead of your circumstances having power over you.

Going back to the professional sports world, that's a highly competitive industry full of athletes with exceptional talent who fail to "make it" and achieve their full potential. It's because these players aren't augmenting their physical talents with the other skills needed for success; largely they lack the proper mindset, discipline, and preparation to give them that edge over the other players out there who are hungrier and who do put in that extra prep work and suit up with the right fundamentals.

Remember we all experience peaks and pitfalls, tragedies, and triumphs. Your life will be full of surprises. It isn't about what is thrown our way that matters, it's how we deal with it that determines who we are and who we become. It's how we respond to every situation in our lives that determines whether we actually move the ball (or not).

If you want things in your life to be different, then the change first starts with you. From your mentality and your attitude to your diet, your sleep, your morning routine, just as how you show up matters, how you suit up matters too.

First, start believing in you and always be willing to bet on yourself, no matter what anyone else tells you. Second, verbalize words of affirmation and confidence daily. Third, choose to bring a positive mindset to the day and continue that positive energy throughout the day so you can move the ball so much further. Fourth, put in the prep work and map out your plan. Keep suited up in positivity and don't let negative outcomes or people deter you from making the day a meaningful one.

COACH'S CHALKBOARD

1. Failing to prepare is preparing to fail.
2. Always stay ready so you don't have to get ready.
3. Your mindset drives your outcomes each day.
4. Practice positive self-talk every morning.
5. Believe in yourself.
6. Radiate positive vibes, all day, every day.

CHAPTER 6:
GIVE YOURSELF PERMISSION

*"It is impossible to live without failing at something, unless
you live so cautiously that you might as well not have lived at
all, in which case you have failed by default."*
—J.K. Rowling

When we decide to start something and put ourselves out there, we tend to focus on the opinions of others and then listen to what they say. Yes, there will be people who will criticize you, who will judge you, who will say you need more work-life balance, who will say it's too risky and that it can't be done. They'll say you can't see clearly. Remember too that those individuals don't see your vision, they don't know your heart, and they will never understand how much that dream means to you.

Of course, it's great to have support from others, but it is better to have a belief in yourself. It's great to have others cheering you on, but it's better to have mental strength. It's great to have people in your corner, but it's better to be able to fight and keep playing when life has you cornered. That starts with putting the following rules into practice.

Rule #1: Give yourself permission to believe in yourself.

In the "Suit Up" chapter, we discussed letting go of your past and forgiving your younger self. Now is the time to believe in your current self so you can create your future self. If you haven't already done so, give yourself that permission today. Often, we can be our harshest critic. Research shows our mind generates between 60,000 and 80,000 thoughts each day and at least 75% of them are negative. That's a lot of negativities! So, it's very easy for your mind to tell you that you can't do something when it comes to venturing into something new or unchartered territory. Doubt and the fear of the unknown and failure will deter you from progressing forward. This little voice within will try to convince you that you cannot realize those dreams that you long for.

You see, this conservative inner voice, wants you to remain in your comfort zone. It doesn't want you to embark on a journey that is unnerving and that will force you to grow. There is no comfort in growth, this is something we know. So your critic within is going to try and stop you from wanting to go for it. This is when you need to be aware of this little voice and tell it to shut up (or maybe you say it in a more polite way). But you need to eliminate those thoughts and give yourself permission to believe in yourself and in your ability to achieve your goals. Push yourself into that gray zone of uncertainty and get comfortable with the unfamiliar. Don't let that voice tell you otherwise. Don't forget your self-talk.

> The most important habit you should develop is the ability to always believe in yourself."
> —Lewis Howes

Rule #2: Give yourself permission to bet on yourself and go after what you want in life.

That risk you are afraid to take, yeah you know which one I'm talking about, could be the one that changes your entire life. When you're willing to bet on yourself, that fear goes away and you're driven to take those risks and see where the journey takes you. It might not take you where you wanted to go, but it could also get you a step or two closer, maybe even more, and further down the path that you need to be. Also, if you're serious about changing your life or achieving the outcomes you desire, when you give yourself that permission to bet on yourself, you will drop the excuses and you'll find a way to get to where you want to go.

Betting on yourself goes hand in hand with confidence; my definition of confidence again being a belief in your ability to figure things out. That doesn't mean you have all the answers, and it doesn't mean that you never doubt yourself. What this means is you believe you can find a solution and take on any obstacle or challenge that comes along your way. You'll get the answers to the things you don't know, you'll come up with creative ideas to tackle a problem. That's how I want you to view the term confidence. You see, when you look at the most high-performing people on the planet, they have that type of confidence. Throw them in any situation and they are convinced that they will be able to handle it. Not because they are the smartest people ever and have all the answers, but because they can bring in the right people, tap into the appropriate resources, and be able to move things forward.

One person who I really enjoy talking about the subject of confidence with is NFL running back, Nyheim Hines. Nyheim first joined me on Season 1 of the *Move the Ball* podcast, and he discussed how key to his continued success in the NFL was his increase in his confidence level. Post this initial podcast episode, Nyheim has continued to dominate on the field and each season he has increased his average yards per carry, a metric that is used, in part, to evaluate a running back's performance. Going back to our podcast, Nyheim said this about confidence:

"Life, sports, everything. It's all about confidence. If you don't believe you're going to do something, you're probably not going to do it. I've even seen players who've elevated their game. We've all seen somebody, it may be a video game or any sport or anything who may be not as good as they think they are, but they're so confident that they play better that what they are or what they should be ... That's how you should be in life. Even if nobody believes in you, you gotta believe in you. And I promise you one thing, if you don't believe in you, nobody else will either. So, it has to start there."

Nyheim continued in the episode discussing how his rookie year he wasn't mentally there. He was young and had never dealt with the business of the NFL and that environment, which was very different than his college years at North Carolina State. But when he changed his mindset and developed more confidence, his performance showed out on the field.

The takeaway is this: confidence and betting on yourself go hand in hand. You can't be willing to bet on yourself, be bold and go after what you want if your confidence level isn't high. Self-confidence is a superpower. Once you start to believe in yourself the magic starts to happen.

Let me share with you another story about one of my good friends, Jalil Johnson, a former NFL defensive back who is currently one of the premiere defensive backs and linebackers trainer in the Houston area. When Jalil was in high school, he didn't have any scholarship offers to play college football. The next stop for him was a junior college. One day, after getting his associates degree, Jalil woke up and decided that he was going to get himself an opportunity to play Division I football. He told his mom and his uncle that he had a meeting with the coaches at Jackson State University (JSU) and convinced his uncle to drive him to the bus stop so he could make the two-hour bus ride to Jackson, Mississippi. The thing was, Jalil had no such meeting with the coaches.

But in Jalil's mind, he was so confident and ready to bet on himself that he was willing to spend his last few dollars on a bus ticket to get to JSU. He knew that if he could just show the JSU coaches his football film and his transcript, they would give him a chance to play. Not having any money for food, for a place to stay in Jackson, or for a return ticket home, Jalil set out on his trip to JSU, full of determination. Once he got to campus, he connected with one of the coaches and sure enough, they gave him an opportunity to be on the team, lodging for the night, and paid for his bus ticket home.

Jalil walked on at JSU, sacrificed a lot (no parties, worked out twice a day, and outworked everyone else on the team), making himself one of the top 50 defensive backs in the nation and then making it to the NFL. Today, Jalil's company, PICK6SIXX, is known as a national brand and players from all over the country, at all levels, come to train with him. This all started because he had the confidence, was willing to bet on himself, and took his shot.

I've always found Jalil's story inspiring, and he and I would always talk about how there are so many people out there who aren't willing to bet on themselves and take that risk. As I previously mentioned, we tend to be our own worst critic. Most people listen to that negative voice. Break yourself from the habit of doing that. Your only limit is you.

Each time that we face our fears, we gain strength, courage, and confidence in doing so. If you hear a voice within you saying, "you cannot *do this*," then by all means do this! Silence that negative, inner voice. People are like stain-glass windows. When the sun is out, they will sparkle and shine. But when the darkness sets in, their true beauty will only be showcased if there is light shining from within. If you are one who has struggled with self-confidence, remember that no one is you and that *is* your power. Loving yourself, believing in yourself, and having self-confidence will enable your superpower and unlock the magic, making "miracles" happen. When you do this, you will not be stopped.

Rule #3: Give yourself permission to be your authentic self.

It is better to fail in originality than to succeed in imitation. Therefore, it is always important that you insist upon being yourself and dare to be different in a world that is full of the ordinary. When you give yourself permission to remain your genuine and authentic self, one that is true to your brand, even if you experience disappointment at times, you will always gain clarity and with clarity comes conviction. As the saying goes, "success is not final, and failure is not fatal."

The road to success and the road to failure are almost exactly the same. But it is through the hard work, perseverance, learning, studying, sacrificing and most of all, the love of what you are doing, that puts you on the path to achieving true success. So, stay true to yourself, yet always be open to learn. Work hard and never give up on your dreams, even when nobody else believes they can come true but you.

These are not cliches but rather real tools you need no matter what you do in life to help you to keep moving forward. Don't trade your originality and your authenticity for safety and comfort. In the end that will not lead to happiness but inexplicable grief. You need to embrace those things that make you unique and showcase your gifts to the world. Giving yourself permission to be authentic is the best gift you can give yourself.

Rule #4: Give yourself permission to fail.

One of the most devastating circumstances in life revolves around failure. When you pour your heart and soul into an endeavor, a business, or a project, and it fails it feels like life has now just been turned upside down. Everything we once thought we wanted seems to simply disappear into thin air. But wait a minute.

"Fail fast, fail often, fail forward." That's what the world's most successful leaders and entrepreneurs always say. In order to be willing to make mistake after mistake, or "fail" multiple times, you have to give yourself permission to do so.

After one "perceived" failure, most people throw in the towel. They quit. They say "Well that didn't work. Guess it wasn't meant to be!" and they focus on some other goal or go do something else. But the true winners in life and in business are the ones who look at that failure and say, "It's okay," I'm okay with sucking at something. I'm okay with putting myself out there, I'm okay with things not working out the way I want."

They live by this mentality because they realize that failure acts as a necessary stepping-stone towards success. For it is through our greatest failures that we learn more about life, goals, happiness, and who we are today. They shape us in ways that we need to really succeed.

Failure is inevitable and it happens to the greatest leaders. Albert Einstein, one of the greatest philosopher-scientists of our time, didn't speak until he was four-years old and failed his entrance exam to the Swiss Federal Polytechnic school in Zurich, Switzerland. Colonel Harland Sanders, the late founder of Kentucky Fried Chicken, failed in many endeavors and at the age of 65 set out with his famous chicken recipe and only a few hundred dollars to his name in an attempt to sell his franchise chicken model. Over one-thousand restaurants rejected him before one accepted his offer.

Henry Ford, father of the automobile who helped bring transportation to the masses in the United States, bankrupted his first company and his second company also went south after he had a dispute with his business partners. JK Rowling, one of the most successful authors in history, was a single mother on welfare, trying to support her daughter. It took her seven years to write the first *Harry Potter* book and all twelve major publishing houses rejected her book. Actor Sylvester Stallone was so broke that while writing the script for *Rocky*, he had his electricity turned off and had to sell his dog for $25 in order to pay the bill and have the lights turned back on. He was also rejected by over 1,500 talent scouts.

The point in sharing all these examples is that failure always happens when chasing greatness. It's ok. Each of these individuals I mentioned succeeded because they gave themselves permission to fail, continued to push, and always put themselves out there.

When starting something new and venturing out of your comfort zone, it's important to realize that you aren't going to be great at it right off the bat. When a professional athlete starts playing a sport, do you think he or she is automatically going to excel at it? Usually that's not the case. As with any new skill, it requires learning the fundamentals, putting in the work to perfect the craft, and practice. The same is true when you are out there doing something for the first time or even if it isn't a new activity. You're going to not be the best at it in the beginning and giving yourself permission to not know all the answers and to make mistakes is a big part of the battle.

When you've allowed yourself that flexibility, you'll have the nerve to try creative solutions to move you forward. You'll be more daring and aggressive in your approach to projects or business ventures. Will all of them work out? No, of course not. But by allowing yourself that grace it will give you more confidence and courage to try new things. Additionally, by giving yourself permission to let go of the fear of judgment, and not care about others' opinions, you really reach a new level of freedom and confidence that you can go after and try anything. This goes hand in hand with giving yourself permission to fail because often we refrain from trying something because we are afraid of what other people will think and how will they judge us.

When you let go of that fear coupled with a relentless mentality that is not afraid to fail, you will be unstoppable and will get to where you want to go. It might not happen as quickly as you like, but it will happen if you stick with it, show up every day and apply the principles mentioned in this book, and be consistent.

COACH'S CHALKBOARD

1. Winning starts with believing in yourself.
2. You don't need to settle in life.
3. Always bet on yourself. No risk, no story.
4. Always remain true to your authentic self.
5. Don't compromise who you are.
6. Give yourself permission to fail.
7. Then fail fast, fail forward, fail often.

CHAPTER 7:
TACKLE THAT PROCRASTINATION

"There are only two options regarding commitment.
You're either IN or you're OUT.
There is no such thing as life in-between."
—Pat Riley

Procrastination is the silent dream killer. It is also known as opportunity's assassin. Think about this for a minute: *The difference between who you are and who you want to be is what you do.* All of us have hopes, dreams, ambitions, and desires. Some people will realize those dreams, others may come close, and some never will. Why? The difference is in how you show up each day. That's what matters and what sets the first group apart; the consistent action that those individuals take daily. It is this consistency that will get them across the goal line. Consistency and tackling procrastination are critical to being able to move the ball.

When you look at the world's most successful business leaders, multi-millionaire entrepreneurs, and top-level athletes, something they all have in common is their unrelenting work ethic. This level of determination also means they don't procrastinate. They handle what needs to be done, whether they are feeling it that day or not, no matter what task it is. They just get down to business and work.

So, what exactly does procrastination mean? Essentially procrastination means you are not doing what you know you need to do, when you know you need to do it. It's putting things off, because in the short term, it's easier, it's more comfortable, and it's more certain.

Let's face it. It's more pleasurable to be distracted or to indulge yourself in doing something else than it is to sit down and do the actual work to create the outputs that matter when they are needed. Especially if those tasks aren't particularly fun, sexy, or exciting.

Procrastination is a trap that most of us fall into at some point. While this happens to all of us, the real question is: *can you set yourself up so that you do less of it?* The answer to this is yes. You can suit up, procrastinate less, and do what you need to in order to progress forward. By following these seven strategies, and practicing them consistently, you will increase your productivity, improve your clarity, and get more done in your life while worrying less.

Strategy #1: Forgive yourself.

Often, people beat themselves up about what has happened in the past. Thoughts such as "I should have started earlier" or "I always procrastinate; I am such a loser" or "I haven't gotten things done in the past, what makes me think I'll be able to now" only makes things worse. While these latter examples are provided more as an extreme to make my point, some people get so demotivated because they haven't made progress and that lack of progress to date or in the past prevents them from suiting up, showing up, and taking action in the here and now.

Research has shown that forgiving yourself for past procrastination will help you stop putting off working on a task. So, give yourself a break, don't beat yourself up over anything you didn't get done previously. Let that go. Now is the time to focus on what business you need to handle and refrain from any further delay.

One common theme discussed with the successful professional athletes I have worked with over the years is how players can't get caught up in the last play. Whatever happened on that last play is in your head, but you have to get it out of your head and focus on the next play. The same thing is true when it comes to them losing a game. They don't remain fixated on the loss, they let that go, and focus on getting ready for the next game.

The same is true here. So what if you have procrastinated in the past? It's time to get that out of your head. Focus on where you are going now. All that matters is how you are going to show up in the present. Let today be the day you learn the grace of letting go and understanding the power of moving on.

Another thing to consider is that you can use past procrastination to your advantage. How? Determine what went into your avoidance in the first place—was it fear, stress, not having a good understanding of how to progress, lack of accountability, etc.? Then what you do is address those obstacles in the present and future. If, for example, it was fear that contributed to your procrastination, what steps can you take to feel more empowered and less fearful next time around? Something for you to think about. Learn from the past and use those lessons to move forward.

Strategy #2: Focus on your "why."

Procrastinators tend to focus more on short-term gains (avoiding the distress associated with the task or the project), as opposed to long-term results (the stress of not doing it, as well as the consequences of avoiding this task). Instead, one way to avoid procrastination is to try focusing on *why* you are doing this task or working on a particular project in the first place. What are the benefits of completing it? Connect yourself to your purpose and really understand your why. Stay linked to that. When you really feel that alignment with the purpose of doing something, you are more motivated, and you actually get the stuff done. So, focus on the why and the benefits of completing something and you'll procrastinate less.

As Simon Sinek, who I mentioned before and who also authored *Leaders Eat Last* and *Start with Why*, says, "Knowing your why is a key essential to lasting success." The why is your origin or purpose and Sinek emphasizes through his work that we need to connect to our why to feel like we belong and also to connect to our communities and our circles of relationships. Being connected to your why inspires behavior and instills the discipline essential to remain focused on your purpose.

So, you see, when you know the color of your jersey and you are connected to your why, it makes it easier for you to want to work on your goals and not procrastinate. Gaining this clarity of purpose is key to avoiding putting off your goals.

Strategy #3: Break things down.

Sometimes when we set big goals for ourselves, you know those ones that require us to really work and push beyond our boundaries of comfortability, what often happens is we end up feeling overwhelmed and stressed out about being able to achieve the goal. We might add unnecessary pressure on ourselves to try and complete the objective, and the result is that procrastination often follows. Does this sound familiar at all?

Here's the solution. When a task or a goal seems overbearing, break that goal or that task into smaller, more manageable parts. By breaking things down into mini milestones, it also helps with daily visualization. This is a concept I discuss in *Move the Ball* called getting the next first down. It's also a concept I talk about in many of my speaking engagements and content because it's so important. In a nutshell, what that means is you need to break your goals down into smaller, more manageable pieces.

This will help ease those feelings of being overwhelmed with all you have to do to complete the project. And when we feel swamped, intimidated, or overwhelmed, we tend to not take action because it just seems to be too much. If you can break your goals and projects into pieces and focus on getting that next first down, it makes it so much easier to plan, to visualize, and you also see the progress which makes you feel good.

For example, if you want to write a book, you may choose to make an outline, identify each chapter, figure out the sections in the chapters, and then commit to writing one segment at a time. Chunking it down like this will help you feel less overwhelmed and more empowered.

Strategy #4: Plan it out.

I'm sure it comes as no surprise that if you have a plan, you are more likely to complete a goal or a task than if you just decide to wing it. That seems to be common sense, right? The problem is that, as high-performance expert Brendon Burchard has said to me on multiple occasions, "Common sense isn't common practice."

If you want to be effective in getting things done, you need to suit up by putting in the prep work. Meaning, if you don't want to procrastinate on a Monday, then Sunday night what you should do is sit down and do this simple, little thing: *project plan and map out what you are going to do in the days ahead.* This is something we discussed in the last chapter as well.

Let me share a little more on how I do this. I like to plan out my entire week on Sunday. I may adjust things (in fact I likely will), but I at least lay out the initial game plan that Sunday. Then each night before I go to bed, I also do another check and plan out what I'm going to do that next day.

I know this is not a sexy, super brilliant idea. While it's not flashy, it will change your life forever. The better organized you are, the more intentional you will be with your time, and the more productive you will become.

An important point to make here is I don't want you to just write down your to-do lists for tomorrow. That is one element of project planning, but I'm talking about a bigger picture. I want you to be thinking about the massive projects you have coming up. I want you to write out the steps it's going to take—especially the big steps—to accomplish your different duties, with a timeline for each of them, and then work backwards from that point to create tomorrow's to-do or priority lists. But here's what's funny: if your mind can't see completion—meaning you don't know the path, you don't have clarity to fulfill or complete something—then your heart will ask you to pause.

What this means is, even if you're the most passionate, dream-oriented, amazing high performing person in the world, without clarity, you'll find yourself procrastinating. Without clarity, you have no goals, no growth, and no change. As previously mentioned in Strategy #2, make sure you are connected to your why.

Here's another point. Now, you might say, "I'm so pissed at myself. I procrastinate and I even know the next three things I should do."

That's not enough. Knowing your next three steps is not going to cut it. Your mind needs to see all the steps through to completion. That's what we call project planning. It's not super fun, but it's saying to yourself, "This is the big project. Here are the big key activities that have to happen to get it done. Here's a timeline for when those things need to happen."

Then you take those big activities and break them down into tasks, and ultimately, into daily to-dos. It's hard to act when you don't have a complete picture like that; that is when you are more likely to procrastinate.

Let me give you an example. There have been studies conducted where they have timed people on how long it takes them to complete a puzzle. Imagine putting together a puzzle with 500 or 1,000 pieces.

The fastest, most productive time in which people put puzzles together is during the last 20% of time they have.

If you've ever done a puzzle, maybe you've walked by it three or four times for a couple weeks and you don't do anything but put a few pieces together. But as soon as the picture becomes a little clearer, you hunker down and complete it, don't you?

This is what is going on with procrastination. Even if you see the first couple pieces of what tasks you need to complete but can't see where it's going, you will want to stop and focus on something else. You'll be easily distracted.

So, if there's an important project you've been procrastinating on, give yourself the greatest gift. Tonight, sit down with your journal and step it all the way out. Even if you have to make it up, figure out what you think needs to be. Even if you're like, "I'm not sure these are actually the big activities."

It's not about having the perfect project plan; it's about having one that is complete with at least the knowledge and details you currently know. Once you have that initial plan, you'll be ready to take action, knowing that you'll figure things out along the way. Your brain won't get fully into a project or an activity it if you haven't project planned it out. This is a really important step. Don't skip this.

What I do to avoid procrastination each week is I sit down every single Sunday to do my Sunday review. I'll literally step through the entire week of all the major things on my to-do list and in my email. I'll think about the bigger projects and I'll step them all the way through. When I do this, I enter the week more engaged, more joyous and more confident, because I know what is going on and I have my playbook for success for the week. A lot of clients I have worked with keep procrastinating because they haven't stepped through their project plan and mapped out what needs to be done. This one exercise is a game changer and will drastically reduce your desire to put things off.

Strategy #5: Visualize the process.

This strategy is a basic one, but it's effective. In fact, most of the adjustments we need to make in life to be successful are small shifts or getting back to basics for success. This is one of those super simple things to implement.

Remember I said you won't do something if you brain can't see it or hasn't stepped it through? Visualizing the process of completing your project, goals, or tasks is an extremely helpful exercise for overcoming the desire to procrastinate.

What I do to make sure I don't procrastinate is I literally visualize and affirm what I am about to do; I see it in my mind.

If it's Sunday, and I have all these tasks I need to finish tomorrow, I'll sit down and for 20-30 minutes and visualize the next day. I'll step it through and see myself going in the kitchen, doing my normal morning routine, grabbing my coffee, sitting down at the computer, opening that blank page, and happily typing along and working on my content. I'll sense and feel those great emotions of doing my calling as a content creator, as a writer, and as someone who tries to inspire others and help others get closer to their goals.

I'll feel the satisfaction of having a productive day which might include producing some new content and some coaching or consulting calls. I'll feel the power and the joy of finishing a great day of writing and producing content, such as a new podcast episode. I'll imagine myself going to dinner, getting to sit down, and looking at how I moved the ball that day.

I'll imagine myself getting ready for bed and looking in the bathroom mirror with a smile on my face because I had made the day an impactful one.

This visualization technique is one that applies for anything you are looking to do. In fact, I do this same exercise with professional athletes that I work with all the time.

I'll tell them, "I don't want you to just imagine the game. I want you to visualize yourself on the way over to the stadium or arena, getting laced up, walking down to the field, stepping out on the turf, and your feelings while walking around. I want you to tap into that sense that you will have as you are in the game, including that sense that you have when you're getting beaten and how you're going to feel and respond to that."

Visualization: it's a technique that is proven to work. When you engage in this exercise consistently, you'll find that you procrastinate far less because you want to bring those images that you envisioned to reality. So, the day before, or the morning of, visualize the entire process of your day. This will get you suited up with the proper mindset and you'll be energized to perform, and to win the day.

Strategy #6: Socialize your plan.

An important component of being able to tackle procrastination is to socialize your plan or your agenda with other people. Why would that be important?

Let me illustrate with an example. There are usually a lot of people out there trying to lose some weight or trying to aggressively go to the gym, especially at the beginning of each new year. What's the first piece of advice given to them because it's proven by science to work repeatedly? *Get a workout buddy. Because if you have a workout buddy, you'll show up.*

Why does this work? It's harder to procrastinate when your name, integrity, and relationships are on the line. In the workout situation, if you have a buddy there expecting you to show up and go to the gym, in most cases you are going to go, because you don't want to be *that* person that flakes and doesn't do what he or she committed to doing.

Socializing your plan to others for any goal is important, and the people you tell are in a way, like your workout buddies. While they might not be there with you each day to work on your goal, by communicating your agenda to others and putting it out into the world, you are making yourself socially accountable. That is really going to make a difference.

Take writing this book for example. When I got serious about writing, I started telling people about it in all kinds of mediums. I posted about it on social media. I also discussed it on my *Move the Ball* podcast as well as on other podcasts where I was a guest. Did I feel some extra pressure because I was letting others know about it? You bet I did! But I also knew that by sharing this with others, I was attaching my name to a goal, and by now you can probably figure out that if I say I'm going to do something, then I'm going to get it done. So, I wanted that social accountability to keep me on my toes, keep me focused, and to make sure I was showing up and handing what I needed to, so I could get this book written.

For me, I love speaking about what I'm going to work on, because it becomes more real for me to complete. By affirming my plans and sharing them with other people, in its own way, I end up being more productive.

Through my executive and personal coaching work, as well as some business consulting projects, I do know without question that communicating one's agenda or plan is a big issue for a lot of people. Some of these people might be work-from-home entrepreneurs, virtual employees, or stay-at-home parents. Some of them are senior leaders in their companies who do a lot of getting status of projects from employees, but they themselves don't get to talk through a lot of things.

It is so important to speak aloud the reality that you want. While you can certainly look in a mirror and say them to yourself, by sharing your goals and plans with other people and socializing that plan, suddenly you won't procrastinate because you know others have heard about your plans and they are going to hold you accountable by asking you questions about your progress.

Sometimes talking with others makes you even want to do it more. It has been found in psychological studies, just speaking out your goals to others makes it more likely you will take consistent action on those goals. Some of these studies have even been done without other people in the equation. They basically just made someone stand in a booth with a microphone and speak out what they were going to do. What those studies found is people who even spoke it to themselves were more likely to achieve their goals than if they just kept it in their head and didn't speak it out loud.

Let's look at the opposite of this. A lot of people keep things to themselves because they are worried about how they'll look, and they fear judgment, pushback, or some other negative feedback. Because of this, they don't share and therefore don't become socially accountable, and they have no social cheerleaders (because they didn't tell anyone).

When you are worried about what other people will think, your brain then thinks the following:

"Well, if other people are going to think I'm crazy, why should I even do this? I mean it's a risk, so I might look stupid if I do."

Your brain continues thinking "Ok, so why am I even imagining this for myself anymore? And if I shouldn't even imagine this outcome or dream, then why should I even spend any more time planning it out?

But wait. The negative thinking doesn't stop there.

Then your brain tells yourself this "Why don't I just go find something else to do like watch Netflix, or go shopping, or go hang out with some friends?"

What then ends up happening is you take no action and procrastinate or just flat out give up on trying to achieve that goal that you were once excited about.

See how all this ties together?

The point is you already know what you are supposed to do. So, plan things out, establish specific deadlines for completing your tasks and projects, and then tell someone about it who will help you to be accountable.

By establishing an accountability partner, this will be a great way to squash procrastination. You can set up time intervals, either in person or virtually, where you can share your progress. By socializing your goals to someone else or putting them out on social media, you'll be putting the world on notice that you are going to do something and when you do that, you're going to want to suit up and take action so you can then claim success to your friends, family, colleagues, and peers.

Strategy #7: Reward yourself for good behavior.

As parents, we tend to reward our children when they do something good because we want to reinforce the good behavior. Why should it be different for you because you are an adult? It shouldn't. It's important for you to celebrate your progress and the accomplishments along your journey, especially when the task is something you easily could have procrastinated on but chose to be disciplined, stayed locked in, knuckled down, and got the dang thing done.

Taking credit and being happy about progress shouldn't just happen when you cross the goal line. I was recently on a podcast where someone asked me, what do you think about football players celebrating when they make a big play or they get a first down? And what I said was I think it's great. It's important to recognize your progress as it keeps you energized and you are more likely to keep the momentum going when you do.

Previously, in Strategy #3, I discussed breaking down your goals and tasks into smaller portions. It's important to celebrate when you accomplish those smaller chunks. Establish rewards for yourself as a "treat" if you do what you set out to do. The problem with not finishing things is we have energy sometimes to get started and then we let distractions and noise get in our way and we lose focus. So, you only get to pay attention to these other things, and reap these rewards, *if* you get done what you need to do.

For example, do not let yourself binge that new Netflix show, check your social media, or get lunch until you complete what you've scheduled. So instead of using these items and distractions as reasons to procrastinate, make them contingent on you finishing your scheduled tasks. Tackling procrastination requires you to be intentional and disciplined and you only get rewarded when you finish the identified items.

There you have it: seven strategies to help you tackle and overcome procrastination. When you put these strategies into practice, you are going to be able to resist the temptation to put off your goals and other activities. It starts with forgiving yourself and giving yourself some grace. Whatever you haven't accomplished in the past, let that go. Stop beating yourself up about the past. There's no reason to think about why you didn't start sooner. Now, just spend your time and energy on moving forward and getting this project done.

Remind yourself why you want to do all of this in the first place. If you stay connected to your purpose, that will keep you focused and driven to perform. By breaking down your project into smaller pieces, it will make things seem more manageable and be energized to make forward progress.

Plan your day the night before to get a head start or at the beginning of the week. Knowing your next steps will help eliminate anxiety and procrastination. Visualize yourself through each step of the process for each day as this will also help you generate excitement for what you are doing, increasing the likelihood that you'll complete it. Socialize your agenda with other people by sharing your goals and timeline for completion. If you speak it, then it becomes more real.

Lastly, it's important to recognize and celebrate your progress along your journey. This will give you energy and momentum to keep going.

Procrastination is a thief of time. Remember that once your time is spent, you can never get it back. The most effective way to accomplish what you want in life is to get uncomfortable, take the first step, embrace the suck, get out there, and be like Nike: *Just do it.*

COACH'S CHALKBOARD

1. The penalty for procrastination is the loss of hopes and dreams.

2. Forgive yourself for your past inactions and start making plays happen today.

3. Remain connected to your purpose as that will fuel you to move forward.

4. Break down your big goals into smaller portions.

5. Project plan all of it out and visualize the process for each day.

6. Communicate your goals to the world. Use social accountability.

7. Recognize and celebrate your progress. Reward yourself often.

CHAPTER 8:
DITCH THOSE OLD CLOTHES
IN THE LOCKER ROOM

"Winning is a habit. Unfortunately, so is losing."
—Vince Lombardi

*M*e *vs. Me. You vs. You.*

Look on social media and you will see competitive athletes constantly posting about the need to outwork yourself, to stop comparing yourself to others, and how the only competition that you need to worry about is you. *"Getting 1% better every day,"* they say.

But here's the thing. To focus on that continual, incremental improvement, fundamentally what first needs to be examined, assessed, and addressed are your *current* habits. Many of us understand that it is your daily routines and habits that ultimately shape your reality and determine the outcomes that you have in life. The problem is that while most grasp this concept, many don't put into place the right habits needed to obtain the outcomes they desire.

As the quarterback of your own life, it is up to you to take complete ownership over the "game" you are playing, focus on what you can control, and take daily action to get you closer to and across your goal line. That daily action includes being deliberate with how you show up to each day. It means consciously and continuously engaging in behaviors that lead to habits that lead to your desired outcomes. It means being purposeful with how you spend every single minute (this will be discussed further in "Manage the Game Clock").

When you want to reach that next level and have a different lifestyle for yourself, it starts with you moving differently. Old keys won't unlock new doors. Old habits won't lead you to where you want to go next. The habits you have put into place previously have gotten you to where you are today, but they aren't necessarily the habits that will get you to where you want to go tomorrow.

I've coached clients who are at various stages in their career and have differing goals and aspirations. When some of them first approached me about wanting to work together, some of them would say, "Jen, I don't know what to do. I'm feeling stuck."

Let's unpack what this really means. There's a difference between having a lack of clarity or a lack of goals and of feeling stuck and not knowing how to move forward. If they are unclear on their vision or their purpose, then we start working together and figure out exactly what jersey they are wearing, what game they want to play, and then we develop a strategy to get across that goal line and to win.

But if it's a situation where these individuals have a goal identified and they are feeling "stuck," what I tell them is they aren't really stuck. Rather, they've just been committed to certain patterns of behavior because those have helped them in the past. But now those behaviors have become more harmful than helpful. That's the reason why they can't move forward. It's because they keep applying an old formula to a new level in their life. This is what I tell them: *You need to change the formula to get a different result.*

In other words, using a sports reference: *You need to ditch those old clothes (i.e. old habits) in the locker room.* It's time to suit up and show up with a new perspective and some new clothes on.

Take a minute and think about your daily patterns. Are you playing the game of life intentionally or are you simply trying to get through the day-to-day and endure whatever life throws at you? Are your daily habits causing you to evolve or revolve? Are you moving forward or just moving in circles? Habits are a critical component to success. Good habits practiced consistently will get you to where you want to go. Conversely, old bad habits are going to prevent you from moving forward.

It's important to take a hard look at your regular practices, be very honest with yourself, and identify what habits are serving you well and which ones are not. Make a list of your current habits and put them in two categories: *habits that are helpful* AND *habits that are detrimental.* You obviously want to keep the ones that are beneficial and ditch the other ones. Then think about your current goals and determine what other behaviors you need to implement in your daily and weekly routine to help you achieve those goals.

Take a simplistic example. Let's say you have a goal of losing ten or twenty pounds over the next few months. An assessment of your current habits includes drinking three cups of coffee daily (loaded with cream and sugar), working out once a week, late night snacking, sleeping an average of seven hours each night, and drinking eight 8-ounce glasses of water each day. Those former three should go in the detrimental habits column while the latter two would fall in the category of helpful habits.

Once you've grouped your existing behaviors, then you need to figure out what other practices would serve you well for this goal. Some questions you might ask yourself are:

- *How could I eat healthier, and what do I need to do to ensure I'm consuming my desired caloric intake for my weight loss goals?*
- *I know I need to exercise more frequently, how often do I need to get a workout in, for how long, and what kind of exercises do I need to focus on?*

- *How can I free up more time to devote towards my health and to work out? What activities do I need to stop so I can get more exercise into my schedule?*

- *How can I change my eating patterns so that I am no longer snacking late at night?*

These are examples of the types of questions to think about for this basic scenario. The questions will obviously vary depending on your objective, but the point of asking yourself questions like these is that the answers will lead you to determining what other habits need to be put into place to best position you for the results that you desire.

When retired NFL quarterback Jason Campbell joined me as a guest on my *Move the Ball* podcast, Jason shared how football taught him resiliency in all aspects of his life. He also discussed the importance of implementing the right habits to enable success. Jason played college football at Auburn University, was drafted in the first round of the 2005 NFL Draft (as the 25th overall pick), and he played in the NFL for ten seasons with the Washington Redskins, Oakland Raiders, Chicago Bears, Cleveland Browns, and Cincinnati Bengals.

During our show together, Jason discussed a recent conversation he had with college football players about integrity and how that comes from within. He talked about if you aren't showing up the right way, things shouldn't feel right, and it should bother you because you didn't put your full effort forward. This is exactly how you should feel about how you're showing up to each day if you haven't been implementing the right habits in your life to get you to where you want to go.

Jason continued on to say, "Every time you have an opportunity to get better, take advantage of that day to get better. We can all find something to complain about. We can all find some reason, someone to blame and all this type of stuff. At the end of the day, you have to look at yourself in the mirror and know what you are doing and why you are doing it and is it enough. Are you doing enough? If you can answer those questions truthfully then you learn more about yourself during the hills and valleys, then on the straightaway."

> 66 *At the end of the day, you have to look at yourself in the mirror and know what you are doing and why you are doing it and is it enough. Are you doing enough?"* —Jason Campbell

Jason is correct in that you have to be focused on how you can get better and improve each day, which includes your habits. How are you suiting up each morning? What are you doing in that first hour once you get out of bed? Are your mornings productive? How much time are you wasting on social media? How often do you get distracted? How can you be more effective with your time? These are all questions you should be answering as you are examining your habits and the shifts you need to make in your daily and weekly routines. You also need to consider, *are you doing enough?*

This is an important question especially when you are dealing with situations of uncertainty or adversity. One thing is for certain: life will throw twists, turns, and curveballs your way. It's often when you don't expect it and likely adds complications and stress in your life. It is during these times that you need to stay focused on the habits that are going to help you get through that situation and make sure you are doing enough and showing up the right way to help you overcome the obstacles and challenges that you might be facing. You can't always predict or dictate the events and outcomes that happen in life, but you can always remain in control of your thoughts, your actions, and your responses.

One other important point to mention is that successful people show up to life ready to achieve excellence over the long term, meaning they are here to play the *long game*. This means setting themselves up for a life of excellence, not exhaustion or mediocrity. Those who play the long game don't compromise in the short term because they know that type of behavior will catch up with them later. This is critical to highlight because as you're ditching those old clothes and replacing them with new ones, you want to make sure you aren't setting yourself up for burnout.

One common mistake people make is thinking burnout is due to one thing or one event setting someone over the edge. This is the farthest from reality. Burnout happens because of little decisions over a period where you are overcommitting your time, don't set boundaries, and are overexerting yourself, resulting in you getting burnt out and feeling completely drained.

Once you've reached this state, it takes a lengthy amount of time to recover. As an example, people keep going hard in the short term so they can achieve an objective. They then hit exhaustion and, consequently, are down for the count for at least a few days. It might be even longer. Sound familiar?

Ok. I'll be one here who takes ownership and raise my hand here. I'll admit that I've experienced this earlier in my career. It's not fun. Let's face it, burnout is a bitch! Exhaustion is a monster that knocks you down for much longer than you want to be out of the game. This is another topic I train on and work on with my coaching clients as the focus is on excellence, not running yourself ragged to get some near-term gain.

It should be clear that by now that you need to be in this to play the long game and not just take what shows up across your path each day. This means architecting or quarterbacking your future, not simply playing in "survival mode." What I mean by that is you can't focus simply on what's in the here-and-now and doing the bare minimum to get through the day and to survive. Winning involves thinking strategically and positioning for the longer term.

To achieve this continuous and sustainable success, you need to take control over your circumstances by focusing on the habits, practices, and routines that will get you across that goal line. Establishing and exhibiting positive habits will help you to get organized, stay focused, and help you whiz through the tasks you need to complete each day. The more structured you are in your regular habits, the easier it becomes to feel accomplished and satisfied every day too.

The thought of changing habits can be uncomfortable and daunting. But change is necessary if you want to reach that next level and have the future that you want for yourself. When people have a big goal or a huge dream, a lot of times they are super motivated. They're excited to get going on that goal and they know what habits need to change to accomplish the goal. They really want to make the change and have great intention, but then they struggle with the implementation.

I am asked quite often, "Why is it that I can't make change stick?" or people share how they have started towards changing their behaviors, but they fall off momentum and just don't keep at it. As discussed in "Own Your Game," you have to own this change, can't be casual about it, and be fully committed to implementing these habits in your life.

This means you can't be half out, be 100% all in. This requires working on the 100% mental commitment. Be sure you are writing down your goals, writing down the habits that you are going to work on, and then mentally commit to this change. Then focus on this daily. Lack of daily attention and continual focus is another reason why people fail in implementing new habits over the longer-term.

Life is full of distractions, from our cell phones to social media to television and Netflix. There are so many things competing for our time and distracting us. If you have children, that's a whole other layer of complexity and demand on your schedule. You can't lose sight of the need to remain locked in on these habits and of holding yourself accountable. Those are necessary steps if you want to be successful and win. Don't let distractions get in your way of practicing your daily and weekly habits.

Ditching these old clothes in the locker room might seem difficult at first. But by giving yourself permission to go after what you want and what you deserve in life will help you stick with making these shifts. Change isn't always fun at first, but if you are serious about your goals, plunge into it, move with it, and then be consistent with it. James Clear, the author of *Atomic Habits*, wrote "Changes that seem small and unimportant at first will compound into remarkable results if you're willing to stick with them for years."

That is the key. You must stick with it. When you show up with these "new clothes" on and perform consistently, you will see the results you are looking for in life and you'll continue to do what you need to move the ball. Let's go. You've got this!

COACH'S CHALKBOARD

1. It is your daily habits that will determine your outcomes in life.

2. Take inventory of your current habits and identify what is helping you and what is detrimental to your progress.

3. Train yourself to let go of things and habits that don't move you closer to your dream life.

4. Ditch those old clothes.

5. Your new habits done consistently will lead you to success.

CHAPTER 9:
GET INSIDE THE HUDDLE

"Surround yourself with only people
who are going to lift you higher."
—Oprah Winfrey

Football—It's a team sport. So is life. In football, a talented quarterback cannot win the game alone. In your game, neither can you. On game day, when the players step onto the football field, energy consumes the stadium. The moment of truth has come. While no one can ever predict the outcome with 100% certainty, one fundamental principle will always hold true: *The players need each other and must play like a team if they want to win.*

Those teammates get inside the huddle, align on the plays they are going to run, and then focus on their execution to move the ball.

If you are familiar with my story, then you know that I fell in love with the game of football when I was four years old. One of the things that hooked me back then was the fact that on any given Sunday, any NFL team could win. Division standings didn't matter, season records were irrelevant. On game day, any team could pull off a victory.

Your situation is no different. Even when crossing the goal line seems impossible, you can make it possible, despite the odds. How many times have you seen the underdog pull off a win in a football game or other sporting event? It happens more often than you think and throughout this book I've shared several examples of this.

As a University of Alabama alumna and passionate college football fan, I want to share another football story with you, one that I cringe at the thought of. But it drives home my point, so here we go.

In November 2012, the Texas A&M Aggies football team was ranked #15 in the nation in college football standings. As the new kid on the Southeastern Conference (SEC) block, Texas A&M quarterback Johnny Manziel prepared for his team's match-up against the defending BCS National Champions and the nationally ranked #1 team, the University of Alabama Crimson Tide.

At the time, Bama was undefeated. Texas A&M had already lost two games earlier in the season. College football fans tweeted their certainty that the Tide had this game in the bag. The Aggies had been 1–10 against top-ranked college teams with their only win coming from a 30–26 victory over the Oklahoma Sooners in 2002. Alabama had won two of the prior three BCS National Championships. The winner in this bout was obvious, right?

On that tenth day in November, over one-hundred thousand enthusiastic football fans poured into Bryant-Denny Stadium in Tuscaloosa, Alabama. Fans with crimson-and-white face paintings were eager to see Alabama blowout another team, a result that the Tide had already delivered on twice previously in the season.

It was game time. The offense started off strong, scoring three touchdowns in the first quarter. The team was moving the ball. But that team wasn't Alabama. Oh no. Manziel, also known to Texans as "Johnny Football," was the playmaker getting the ball into the end zone. The Aggies were dominating. At half-time, they were still up by six.

Manziel and his offense kept the plays alive, while the A&M defense pressured Alabama during the second half. The Aggies had the lead and wanted to keep it. This required playing strong football until the game clock expired. For as we all know, the game isn't over, until it's over.

Alabama's quarterback, AJ McCarron, nearly pulled off a comeback for the Tide in the fourth quarter. With 1:36 left in the game, McCarron threw a pass for what would have been a game-winning touchdown. But the defense prevented the pass completion. The clock ticked down to 00:00. Final score: Texas A&M 29, Alabama 24. The underdog had won.

For the entire sixty minutes of regulation, the Aggies were in the huddle, knuckled down as a team, and played a solid game. This was key to their success. Manziel couldn't do it alone and leveraged the strength of his teammates to pull off the upset.

On that Saturday, the Aggies had played with heart and remained relentless. Their drive paid off and Texas A&M was the winner of a key SEC showdown. They didn't let current college football rankings or season records distract them from playing solid football and handling their business. They had proven so many wrong that day and held their heads high as they ran back into the locker room victorious.

Alabama finished their season with a 12-1 record and went on to a repeated BCS National Championship. A friend of mine who played on that Alabama team and went onto play in the NFL for five seasons, Quinton Dial, said this about that game, "I definitely learned a lesson that day."

Johnny Manziel finished the season as the winner of the Heisman Trophy, the most prestigious award bestowed in college football. Texas A&M was proud of their feat that day and this game is one that gets mentioned even to this day. Beating Alabama was no easy feat and there is no shortage of players who love to remind me of a time when their college team beat Bama.

Life is like football in that it can be filled with highs, lows, turnovers, fumbles, and uncertain outcomes. There will be times you feel like the underdog. However, similar to Texas A&M, you can win against the odds. But you need a team to do it. You need to get inside the huddle with a squad of people who know how to move the ball and make things happen.

Who and what we surround ourselves with shapes the outcomes we have in life. Each day when you suit up and show up, you should be clear as to what jersey you are wearing and what specific goals you are striving to achieve. You also need to identify who your playmakers need to be to take on extraordinary feats. It is time to build out your roster and bring key players into the huddle.

It's important to have people in your circle who are excited about your ambitions. They may be people who aspire to achieve the same goal. Or they might simply be supporters ready to keep you motivated. Either way, you need to know who these individuals are, what their role is, and how they will continue to provide you with moral support and positive energy when uncertain times test your resolve.

To make sure you have the right people on your team, follow these rules so you know who you can pull inside your huddle.

Rule 1: Make sure your team has the "It Factor."

If you truly want to be successful and reach that next level of greatness, you need to surround yourself with what your version of success looks like. What does "winning" mean to you? How have you defined it? Hint: You should know the answer to this already, but if not, then make it an action item to figure that out today.

An important component of being able to achieve exceptional things is to surround yourself with people who are going to lift you up, bring out the best in you, and challenge you to become the best possible version of yourself each day. On the *Move the Ball* podcast, one of the common themes I hear from professional athletes is that a key to their success was that they surrounded themselves with teammates who were more skilled than them, who they could learn from, and who would help them excel.

This isn't just true in football. Oh no, this applies off the field and beyond the game in all settings. Make it a priority to align yourself with people who want to be more, do more, and strive for more in life. You want people in your huddle that have the "It Factor."

Let me explain this concept by sharing a story with NFL Defensive Back, Shyheim Carter, who played college football at The University of Alabama and was a member of the 2017 CFP National Championship team. When Shyheim was in high school, like many other talented athletes, he played both sides of the ball.

During his junior and senior years, Shyheim earned Class 1A Offensive MVP and as a senior he tallied 57 tackles and five interceptions on defense. But wait, there's more! During that same year, Shyheim had 2,443 passing yards, 1,648 rushing yards, and 30 combined touchdowns on offense, ultimately leading his school, Kentwood H.S., to its first state title since 1998. As a top cornerback in the nation and ranked #114 in the Rivals250 in 2016, Shyheim had top schools such as Alabama, Louisiana State University (LSU), Ole Miss, and Miami, looking to recruit him to play college football.

Shyheim chose Alabama. When I asked him why, he told me that "Bama had that 'It Factor.'" People asked him all the time why, as a kid from Louisiana, he didn't go to LSU or some other school. They wanted to know what he thought made Alabama so special for him.

> *Whether I was sitting in the locker room or I was sitting in meeting rooms, I would be sitting with first round players at my position."*
> —Shyheim Carter

As a guy who hated to lose and thought of himself as a winner, Shyheim's rationale for making the decision to play for the Crimson Tide came down to he wanted to surround himself with people who knew how to win. He would not only get the proper coaching from a coaching staff that had built a culture of excellence, but he would be, according to Shyheim, "coached by the best and play underneath the best . . . I was going to get first round players every day at practice."

You see this "It Factor" that drove Shyheim to choose Alabama over other schools was because he knew he would be around people that were stronger, faster, and better than him. He appreciated that to win a national championship and develop into a player that could make it to the next level in the NFL, the people he interacted with daily needed to be people who knew how to win, had a history of winning, and were part of program that attracted the best talent.

Alabama certainly met those criteria when Shyheim was transitioning from high school to college, and it still meets that criterion today. In fact, prior to the 2021 college football season, Alabama had 18 national championships under its belt. Not only does Alabama have a strong track record for winning, but the football program also does a phenomenal job of attracting and cultivating talent to play football at the next level. If you weren't aware, Alabama ranks in the top ten schools producing the most NFL players in NFL history. Furthermore, in 2018, 2019, 2020, and 2021, Alabama had the most players on NFL rosters and holds the record (tied with Ohio State) for the greatest number of players to be drafted in the 2021 NFL Draft (10).

Clearly Alabama knows what excellence looks like, possesses that "It Factor," and was the reason Shyheim chose to go there. Shyheim considered himself a winner and wanted to play for a school that would help him win a Natty. That he did, by being a part of Alabama's 2017 National Championship team.

Now the takeaway for you with this is that you need to evaluate the people who are currently on your team and determine whether those are the right players. As they say, you are the average of the five people you hang around. Who are you interacting with on a daily and weekly basis? Are they the winners that can help you get across the goal line? Or do you need to make some changes?

You've probably heard the saying that if you are the smartest person in the room, then you are in the wrong room. This is so true. The only way you are going to level up is by aligning yourself with people who are better than you, smarter than you, and have done the things that you have set out to accomplish. You need people who have that "It Factor."

When I was getting ready to leave my corporate job to focus on growing the Move the Ball movement and become a full-time entrepreneur, most of my colleagues and friends were executives and senior executives in big corporate environments. If you've ever been an entrepreneur, or worked in a small start-up environment, you know working in that space is extremely different than a Fortune 100 or Fortune 1000 company.

Since I was making a drastic adjustment to my future, I knew the people inside my huddle needed to be changed too. I needed to find entrepreneurs who had that "It Factor." What that meant was not just finding anyone who considered themself a successful entrepreneur because they had survived a few years and were still chugging along. No, I wanted to align myself with those entrepreneurs who had built successful, global brands. You know, individuals who had built businesses with $100M+ valuations or more. Those kinds of people because I wanted to learn what they did and didn't do to succeed in this space.

Afterall, entrepreneurship was a game I had never played. Having an MBA, being an attorney, and having significant corporate experience,

I was sure I had the business savvy to be successful as an entrepreneur. But I had massive goals and dreams and wanted to not just get by. Oh no, I wanted to build something extraordinary. This was going to be my legacy after all. To do that, I needed to surround myself with a team of exceptional people. I needed teammates who would challenge my assumptions, really push me into uncomfortable spaces and try non-traditional approaches to continue to level up, and force me to think even bigger. Go big or go home, right?

> " Great teamwork is the only way we create the breakthroughs that define our careers."
> —Pat Riley

This was my mentality and so I sought out those who really were winners, weren't afraid to take risks, and had crossed the goal line. Those who had scored touchdowns many, many times.

Whatever your goals might be, it is an absolute must that you bring people into your huddle who aren't just cheerleaders, but rather are people who have that "It Factor," are more experienced and skilled than you, and can really help you to make forward progress and to win.

Someone once told me this, which is something I've passed onto other people. He said, "If you hang around 5 confident people, you will be the 6th. If you hang around 5 intelligent people, you will be the 6th. If you hang around 5 millionaires, you will be the 6th. If you hang around 5 idiots, you will be the 6th. Who are you hanging around?"

This is a question you need to ask yourself, and then make adjustments if needed.

Rule #2: Get yourself some mentors and sponsors.

In addition to having people that possess that "It Factor," you need to find people who can be mentors and sponsors. It's important to note that some of the people that fit into this category can be people who you think possess what I described above. But a distinction between this group and the first group is the frequency of your interactions. The individuals I described above are your day-to-day "go to" people who you are in constant communication with.

Mentors and sponsors are people who you talk with on a periodic basis, but they aren't focused on the nitty gritty details of what you are working on from week to week. A mentor is someone who you can develop a long-term relationship with that is centered around building your professional career or your business growth and development.

Again, a mentor is not there to work with you on a daily basis to help you make decisions, but they are there to serve as someone who can offer support, wisdom, and share their knowledge and experience with you. While you don't include them in your frequent and on-going communications, you can lean on mentors to also help you work through a critical decision or to get their opinion on how you should proceed. Mentors also tend to be well-connected and can introduce you to their professional network and help set you up for success in your career and business endeavors.

A distinction worth making here is a mentor should not be confused with a coach. A coach is someone who focuses on specific strengths and weaknesses. The relationship with a coach and their client tends to be more finite in nature, while a mentor/mentee relationship tends to be long-term and less structured. There are circumstances where you might be looking for a coach to develop a certain skillset, or work on your strengths and weaknesses, such as an interview coach, a public speaking coach, an executive coach, a business coach, or a fitness coach. These can be valuable resources to explore as part of your huddle too.

Lastly, another group of individuals you need to have in your circle is sponsors. A sponsor differs from a mentor in that a sponsor is a professional at a higher level (usually internal to the company if you are in corporate) who can support and promote you. They are your champions who will advocate on your behalf as to why you are the best person for a role. In other words, sponsors use their influence or leadership status to advocate for your advancement or provide you with access to opportunities. They are going to actively promote you, put your name forward for high-stakes assignments, and spend their political capital to work your name into conversations.

During my corporate career, I was fortunate to climb the corporate ladder pretty quickly. While there were several factors I would attribute to that success (hard work, differentiated value, performance, etc.), having sponsors in my corner also helped me land opportunities and be more visible to senior executives. Those sponsors not only elevated my visibility at work but placed me in new roles, ensured I got credit, and backed me in my absence during career conversations.

Winning a sponsor is not a straightforward process and you can't just randomly ask someone to be you sponsor. You need to show up to work with an ambitious attitude, be eager to volunteer to take on projects, and develop a reputation as being someone who significantly contributes to teams and to the company. Being willing to take on riskier and more challenging projects and tasks is also a good way for people to see you in action (including senior leaders) which opens the door for you to approach them and ask if they would be willing to become a sponsor and advocate for you in the future.

Rule #3: Assess, evaluate, and grow your network.

You probably have figured out that you become what you focus on and are shaped by the people you spend time with. Your network is your net worth, so you want to make sure you are keeping it as strong and valuable as possible. That network should include people who have the "It Factor," who have the experiences and insights that can help you to accelerate your progress, who are sponsors and mentors, and also friends, colleagues, and co-workers who you can trust and who are cheering you on. You should also always be looking to learn from people you meet, as this can speed up your game plan as well.

If you already have a strong network in place, that is great. Keep those teammates out there on the field with you. If you do not have as robust of a network as you would like, then make it a priority to build your team. Identify what type of support and experience you need. Then draft your players.

It is important to note that you will have different people in your huddle for your different goals. This is how it should be. The people on your team for your business goals likely won't be the same people for your fitness objectives or your side hustle plans. You can think of it like fantasy sports where you will likely draft different players for the different fantasy teams you have.

No matter what your goals are, to win and be successful in business and in life, you need to get yourself connected. This was something that served me well when I was working in corporate as well as when I ventured off into my current entrepreneurship ventures working with corporate executives, professional athletes, and business owners.

Many years ago, when I worked at General Electric, I had been there a little over a year when my then boss, Gerry, who was Vice-President of Strategic Initiatives for GE's Avionics business, told me I was one of the most connected people in the company he knew.

While he made an interesting observation, it didn't exist by accident. Getting networked had always been an essential part of my playbook. I understood the importance of building different teams. I recruited players who would help me accomplish my varying business and career objectives.

Relationships go a long way. Don't underestimate them. You need people in your life who are going to lift you higher and take your game to the next level. Life is not a solo game. Don't play it as if it were. Remember to periodically revisit who you have in your huddle and who is in your network. You always want to continue to grow that network with the right people and keep it as strong as possible.

Rule #4: Make sure you know who your supporters and cheerleaders are.

Not everyone who wants to see you win in life is playing the same game as you. They might be on another field focused on other dreams and aspirations. What this means is that while these people won't be in your huddle as you are out there navigating the day-to-day, they are still important and should remain part of your squad. Don't forget about them or ditch them just because they are pursuing other endeavors. Supporters are important, you need them too.

You will want to continue to share your progress with your friends and co-workers that you have supportive relationships with. Their passion for success will also drive you forward toward your goal line. By communicating your goals with your supporters, you are putting your goals on the record. These players will listen to you, keep you grounded, hold you accountable, and share their experiences with you.

Your supporters will keep you driven and energized to succeed. A study found that people who did weekly email updates with friends were thirty-three percent more likely to score successes than those who just formed goals. To be successful in life, you must include people in your line-up who simply want you to win. They may or may not have experiences or relevant advice they can pass onto you, but they can lend their emotional support. You need your cheerleaders too, and their encouraging and positive energy!

Publishing *Move the Ball* was a remarkable adventure for me. It was initially a little intimidating too. Becoming a published author had been my dream for over a decade. While my book ideas had changed over the years, the vision was to write a professional development and inspirational type of work. To be completely transparent, the reason I didn't publish a book sooner than I did was because every time I headed down that road, I allowed myself to make excuses.

I told myself, "It's not the right time," or convinced myself that life was too crazy at the moment. Here's a hint: As we get older, life doesn't get any less complicated. There is never going to be that perfect time. So really, you just need to start something new now. No more procrastination and no more excuses.

Over the years, I was apprehensive and unsure of my way forward. This was unfamiliar territory and it was comfortable for me to stay in my current lane. It was easier to just *do nothing* and continue to kick the can down the road. I could have chosen never to step onto the field and play the game, but I finally decided that I was going to be 100% committed and see my dream of publishing a book through to the end.

When I wrote *Move the Ball*, my mindset was different. I was locked in and not going to allow myself to make excuses. I shared my goal with a few of my close friends, two (Johnie and Todd) were my initial big supporters, neither of whom were interested in publishing a book at the time. While we had differing goals, they were there to help me continue to progress forwards.

I walked through outlines and chapters with them. They gave me feedback and suggestions on how to improve. Both Johnie and Todd understood my passion for football and my desire to write about the life lessons the game had taught me. Throughout the years of knowing each other, we had spent countless hours analyzing football games, trades, and draft picks. Of course, we also bitched when our teams lost. I got to hear Johnie, an Ole Miss grad, grumble often. There was this one time though, that Johnie also got to rub it in when Ole Miss beat Bama in 2015. He was happy about that!

Both Johnie and Todd were fired up about me writing my book. They held me accountable and encouraged me to keep moving towards the goal line. The support was energizing and inspiring.

Over time, I brought others into my huddle. I worked full-time at GE and part-time as a JAG officer in the Michigan Army National Guard while writing *Move the Ball*. I also had four children living at home. Life was busy. Getting 110% support from my teammates motivated me to keep going.

I had a game clock and kept measuring my progress on the field. I knew how much time was left to get into the end zone before my deadline hit and kept taking daily action to make things happen. Having my supporters and people cheer me on helped keep me going.

I cannot stress the importance of you having a group of positive people cheering you on and celebrating your progress towards your goals. Their energy will help you continue to show up and keep pushing, especially on the days when you are not feeling it—you know those days where you aren't in the mood or those days that seem like they might be turning into "bad days."

Rule #5: Have the courage to raise your hand.

In business great leaders ask for help early and often. So do elite coaches and players. They are not afraid to speak up and ask for support. You can't be either and shouldn't be apprehensive to raise your hand when you need help. This isn't a sign of weakness, but rather a sign of strength.

As a kid growing up in Chicago, I loved Chicago Bears football.

Many Chicago fans remember when Jim Harbaugh transitioned from being the University of Michigan quarterback to playing professional football. The Chicago Bears had drafted Harbaugh in the first round of the 1987 NFL Draft, as the 26th overall pick, and he played with the Bears through the 1993 season. After playing in Chicago, he continued his NFL career with the Indianapolis Colts, Baltimore Ravens, San Diego Chargers, Detroit Lions, and the Carolina Panthers. He hung up his cleats in 2001.

From 1994 to 2001, while he was still playing in the NFL, he also served as an unpaid assistant coach at Western Kentucky University where his father, Jack Harbaugh, was the head football coach. After serving as a quarterback coach for the Oakland Raiders, Harbaugh returned to college football in head coaching slots at the University of San Diego and then Stanford. In both head coaching roles, Harbaugh had turned around losing teams and made them winners. After leading Stanford to an Orange Bowl victory in 2011, he was hired to be the head coach of the San Francisco 49ers.

During his first season with the team, the 49ers won the NFC West Division Championship. The following season they went to the Super Bowl. While the 49ers lost to the Baltimore Ravens 31-34, Harbaugh's leadership was a strong component in the team's success that year. A few months after that Super Bowl, I had the opportunity to chat with Jed York, CEO of the 49ers' organization. He shared with me that Harbaugh was a leader who was never afraid to ask for help. According to York, "Coach" didn't hide his shortcomings and often sought out others for their expertise, which he felt made Harbaugh a successful coach.

We already know that in life we need a team to help us get across that goal line. But we can't be anxious about sharing our faults or where we need help. No one is perfect and no single person knows the answers to everything. Every player on a football team brings a different skillset to help win the game. In business, every individual on the team is unique and brings distinct talents and perspectives to the game.

If you don't know an answer to something or need expertise that is outside of your wheelhouse, have that courage to ask for help. Not only do people want to contribute, but they will also appreciate that you looked to utilize their capabilities and expertise to help the team.

This is also very important when you are pushing new boundaries, testing new markets, and venturing into unknown territories. Leverage your team often. This will set you up for the maximum possibility for success. Know when you need help and have the courage to ask for it. Throughout my career at Fortune 100 companies, this was a fundamental principle driven home by senior leaders. Asking for help when needed has been a crucial practice for both my personal and career goals.

Achieving your goals starts with you, but they don't happen only because of you. Of course, it starts with how you suit up. You have to believe in yourself and your abilities to accomplish those goals. Then you have to take ownership—have that commitment to the game and confidence to successfully play the game. Get obsessed with winning. Then you've got to surround yourself with people who will help you win.

While you are the quarterback and control the ball, it cannot be just you on the field. If you want to succeed in life, a team of mentors, sponsors, supporters, cheerleaders, and players with the "It Factor" is required. Figure out who needs to be on your roster today. As you keep moving, relook at your goals and your plans. Discover how to use your team to provide you with coverage, keep you grounded, and execute spectacular plays. Put your best team forward, show up to play the game with your winners, and get inside the huddle

PART II: SHOW UP

COACH'S CHALKBOARD

1. The people closest to you will determine how successful you are. Pay attention.

2. Make sure your teammates have the It Factor.

3. Get mentors, sponsors, cheerleaders, and supporters.

4. Bring in a coach to work on specific strengths and weaknesses.

5. Ask for help early and often.

6. Continue to evaluate, assess, and grow your network.

7. Get inside the huddle and use your team to move the ball.

CHAPTER 10:
KEEP YOUR ENGINE TUNED

"You are trying not only to reach your potential but to move beyond it. If you are not in the best shape you can be, these things simply become more difficult to achieve."
—Rick Pitino

It's a nippy winter day in New York City and Sara needs to get from her apartment in Manhattan to Wall Street. Wearing her gray peacoat that covers her business suit with knee-high boots underneath, she hurries down the block to the MTA Subway—33rd Street entrance. Sara stands on a crowded train listening to her iPod as the metro travels past the other Park Place stops, Union Square, Canal Street, City Hall, and finally stops at Wall Street. She then exits from the subway and makes the five-minute walk to her workplace—another uneventful commute in the daily life of Sara McDonald.

Not all of us get to be like Sara with access to efficient public transportation that gets us to work and around town. If you don't live in a major metropolitan area, getting from point A to point B requires another mode of transportation, usually that being a car or some other motor vehicle. And to minimize the likelihood of car trouble while you're driving around, you need to make sure your vehicle is well-maintained and in tip-top condition.

Car enthusiasts are people who especially appreciate the need to keep their cars at their best. You know who these people are in your neighborhood. Look out your window on a sunny summer weekend and you'll likely find these people in their driveway waxing their precious Shelby, Mustang, Z28 Camaro, Corvette, or something similar. That car is their baby, and they will spend hours giving it some tender loving care (good ole TLC). But it's not just car aficionados that should be concerned with automotive maintenance and care.

From oil changes to new air filters, wheel alignments to break replacements, switching out spark plugs to changing the timing belt, all of it is critical to having a well-functioning vehicle. Proper care is a must to ensure your car will perform at its peak for years to come. And then you cannot forget the engine tune-up!

While your car is valuable to you, the most critical possession you own is not your automobile, it's your body. You see, that's the vital apparatus that will help you move the ball. Just as you check in on your car periodically to make sure it's functioning well, you also need to check in on yourself on a frequent basis. In other words, you need to put yourself first and ensure that you are running in great condition; for you'll need to be at your best level if you want to be a high performer and win in life.

When we set challenging goals for ourselves, navigating the journey can be filled with unknowns, uncertainties, speed bumps, roadblocks, and so much more. The path ahead will try your patience and test your resolve. It will stretch you in ways you didn't want to be stretched or know you could be stretched. It will be a complicated road at times, one that will take patience, perseverance, and require sacrifice. Remember though, in the end it will be worth it.

To be successful on this journey, you need to keep your body's engine tuned. That's critical because, remember, you are here to play the long game. Follow these simple rules to keep yourself running at optimum performance:

RULES TO MAKE SURE YOUR ENGINE IS TUNED

1. Put yourself first.
2. Check your numbers.
3. Kickstart your day with a healthy breakfast and follow a healthy diet.
4. Get enough sleep.
5. Never slack on fitness.
6. Control your stress.
7. Don't run yourself ragged.

Rule #1: Put yourself first—make YOU a priority.

When you see a puddle of fluid under your car what do you do? Perhaps you brush it off, thinking it's no big deal? But it could be an oil leak. Maybe it's not. If it is, ignoring this can lead to the complete depletion of oil within the engine parts. This may result in damaged engine components costing you time, money, and headaches. Car problems like this often start out as small incidents. Neglecting these warning signs will turn into bigger, sometimes overwhelming, problems. This is not only true with our vehicles.

As we get older our lives get more complex. Our jobs command more responsibility and we juggle family commitments. Face it—there are more demands for our time. It's an endless cycle. When we get caught up in the rat-race, it's easy to ignore the indicators our bodies may be flashing at us. We don't make time for ourselves and then run into health issues when they become extremely problematic. Neglecting your body and your health comes at a price.

Let's look at Car A that has been well-maintained and never missed a manufacturer-recommended scheduled maintenance interval. Then there's Car B which is the same year, make, and model as Car A. However, Car B's owner does not bother with regular oil changes, air filter replacements, and drives the car aggressively by taking turns faster and hitting potholes at high speeds. By not properly caring for his vehicle, Car B's owner will have a car that may only last for 150,000 miles, whereas Car A's owner should be able to drive the vehicle for well over 200,000 miles before he needs a new car. This is a simplistic example, but it makes my point.

Our minds and bodies are like cars and how we drive them will take a toll. As players in the game of life, we need to be in top-notch shape, which requires making our health and well-being a priority.

When I was in my twenties, I felt like I was running a million miles an hour. Friends and co-workers expressed their concern for how hard I was working myself. "Jen, you need to slow down," they would say.

One colleague shared how he *used* to be like me. Circumstances had been stressful and long hours had taken its toll. Serious health problems surfaced and his doctor cautioned that if he didn't alter his lifestyle, he would be dead by forty. He took that seriously, altered his routine, and focused on his health. He made himself a priority, reduced the stress in his life, and was very healthy and happy as a result.

I cannot stress enough the need to focus on your health and listen to your body. It's imperative that you make time for you and your well-being. Of course, this is easier said than done. Making yourself a priority takes a serious commitment from you. If I can do it, so can you.

During my career, working for Fortune 50 companies was very demanding. There was no such thing as a 9-to-5 day or a 40-hour workweek. Who has these anymore, anyway? I spent countless nights on phone calls and my colleagues often saw emails in their inbox "from Jennifer Garrett" with a time stamp of 2 am. It was the nature of the business and sometimes those things had to be done. However, along with that work-hard culture came the understanding that while there would be long hours, there would be times my teammates and I would also need to unplug to recharge.

A demanding work schedule, coupled with shuffling children to sports practices and other commitments, left little time for pampering and relaxing. However, because I realized the importance of self-care, I always scheduled in some down time to ensure I could recoup, relax, and recharge.

Life's demands make it so easy to lose sight of our needs and how we need to put ourselves first. Making yourself a priority is not selfish. You owe that to yourself and to your family. Take care of you and don't skimp on the "me" time. The need for and importance of taking breaks is something discussed more in "Call the Time Out."

Rule #2: Check your numbers.

In the business world, there are metrics to measure performance. In sports, we use stats to compare players and teams. Numbers are everywhere. When it comes to your health, there are numbers too—critical health indicators that you should be aware of. Do you know what your blood pressure reading is? What about your total cholesterol? Or your fasting glucose, i.e., blood sugar, level? How about those triglycerides?

According to the Center for Disease Control, nearly 94 million U.S. adults aged 20 or older have total cholesterol levels higher than 200 mg/dL. Higher cholesterol levels lead to increased risk of heart disease. Are you one of the 94 million? If you know you fall into this category, what will you do differently to change this and to manage your cholesterol? If your cholesterol level is normal, then keep doing what you are doing. But don't forget to check it periodically. Lastly, if you don't know, then that should be a sign that you need to check your numbers and find out.

Cholesterol level is just one of the many health metrics you should be tracking, blood pressure is another one (as the American Heart Association calls high blood pressure "the silent killer"). If you are unsure of what you should be monitoring, this is something you will want to discuss with your primary care physician at your next appointment. It is important for you to understand what these numbers are, where your measurements fall, and what steps you need to take to bring them into the healthy range.

Rule #3: Start the day with a healthy breakfast and maintain a healthy diet.

If you want to win every day, it not only starts with suiting up the right way with the proper mindset, but also starting off each morning with a big punch so you can be fully energized and ready to take on any obstacle or challenge the day might bring. According to the Mayo Clinic, adults who eat healthy and nutritious meals in the morning are more likely to: control their weight, control their blood sugar levels, and perform better at work.

But it isn't just breakfast that matters. You need to be mindful of everything you are putting in your body. I previously mentioned the MAD PRIDE term and the second D in this acronym stands for *Dedication to a Healthy Diet.* Having a balanced diet is key if you want a strong mind, body, and spirit; it's a necessity to positioning yourself to win. Elite players focus on their nutrition and their diets, and so should you.

In fact, proper nutrition is a topic I frequently talk about with professional and college athletes, as well as performance trainers and coaches. Two such individuals I am often talking about my diet with are NFL Defensive Tackle, Tanzel Smart Jr., and his performance trainer, Derrick Joseph who is the owner of DeeJoe Fitness in New Orleans, Louisiana. As individuals who both know how to move the ball and get stuff done, they appreciate that to be successful and perform at your peak, you don't only need to be physically in shape, your diet is equally as important.

Both of these guys have shared with me how they are firm believers in what you put in your body matters and they always say you can't put regular or bad gas in a car and expect it to go fast. Higher performing cars have to be fueled with higher octane gas. The same is true with being an elite athlete or kick-ass individual off the field. What you put in your body as fuel is important because what you consume affects your output and the outcomes that you'll have each day.

This doesn't mean that everything you eat needs to be super healthy. You can have cheat foods on occasion, but there needs to be a balance and a diet that is more heavily focused on the healthier side. Something funny to share is that because I've talked with Tanzel and Derrick about diet and we've discussed this car analogy, any time I find myself grabbing for a cheat item, I picture Tanzel or Derrick (or both of them) standing next to me just staring as I'm about to shove that unhealthy piece of food in my mouth. Sometimes I'll even pause before eating it because I visualize them shaking their head. When this happens, sometimes I text them to let them know. I'm sure they get a kick out of it!

The takeaway to this rule is you should commit yourself to kicking off your day with a healthy breakfast and integrating a nutritious diet into your daily and weekly schedule. When you do this, you'll notice that you'll have more energy and you'll feel better about yourself too.

Rule #4: Let your brain and your body sleep.

How you show up matters. If you really want to maximize your potential every day, it also starts with making sure you are suiting up with a clear mind and that you've gotten enough sleep the night before. Being well-rested will get your mind ready to focus on the uncomfortable things you need to get done, the tasks you don't want to do, and get you in a state where you are ready to take on whatever challenges the day may bring.

At the beginning of each year, people often create New Year's resolutions. At the start of a new month, people start thinking about their 30-day or their monthly goals. Those might involve losing weight, working out, eating better, stressing less, quitting bad habits, and being more productive.

Many of my coaching clients and people I work with who set these types of goals are surprised to learn how closely sleep relates to achieving most of them. Getting enough sleep is such an important topic for me because over fifty years of research has shown that if you are not getting enough sleep then:

- *Your cognitive abilities throughout the day go down.*
- *Your creativity goes down.*
- *Your stress goes up.*
- *Your bad decision making goes up.*
- *Your ability to handle conflict or life challenges and be resilient, happy, and positive all goes down drastically.*

All of us have many expectations placed on us, and a lot of demands in our lives. At some point many people start believing the hype out there that you can get by on three to four hours of sleep.

"Don't worry about it."

"Just sleep a little less."

"Get up a little earlier."

"Just hustle harder."

These are things we start hearing people say and many start telling themselves this big lie that they can get away with less sleep, even though fifty years of science says that we can't. Most normal people, those people who care about high performance, really need to sleep seven to eight hours a night, according to the experts.

With all the commitments I've juggled in my life—my five kids, my military career, the Move the Ball brand, and the movement, being an entrepreneur, sitting on boards, running coaching programs, and all the other endeavors I'm involved with—people often say "Jen, do you ever sleep?"

The truth of the matter is, yes, I do sleep. I also try to get seven to eight hours of sleep as often as I can. Now that doesn't always happen every single night, but I do it as often as I can because it is so important. If I end up staying up late on certain days during the week, then on weekends if I can, I'll make sure to get that extra sleep in.

Sleep is such a huge priority for me that I make the conscious decision to get it in on a weekly basis and if I need to scale back on commitments or say "No" to projects in order to be able to balance everything and make sure I'm resting, then that's what I do. I also make sure to be super effective with the time I am awake, so I can fit in that amount of sleep into my schedule each week.

If you are only getting four to five hours of sleep, don't stress about figuring out how you're going to get from four to eight hours in a night. Here's where I want you to start. Take the pressure off yourself and just get 45-50 additional minutes of sleep starting tonight. To make this super simple, go to bed 45 minutes earlier than you usually do. It might not seem like much, but this little bit of extra sleep will help start a new habit that could change your life.

Sleep is one of the best ways to support several aspects of health and wellness at once. But being able to get more sleep, like anything else, is a function of what you put into it. Aiming to sleep more will pay off over the next few months and for years to come if you stick with it. All it takes is a little motivation, discipline, and integrating healthy sleep habits into your routine.

Rule #5: Stay fit. Make exercise fun.

You need to be active. It's that simple. If you want to have stamina to endure the trials and tribulations you will go through as you push boundaries and navigate being uncomfortable, you need to be healthy. Remember, this is a marathon and not a sprint; your physical, mental, and emotional stamina will be tested. Making time in your day for physical activity will help keep these three areas strong. It can be as simple as walking with co-workers during lunch time or going for an early morning run.

This should not feel like a chore. If you feel like you are forcing yourself to get active, then you will only do it for a short time. Change up your routine and make it fun. One suggestion is to pick an active outing. Instead of going to the theater, take a date to the park or to a roller-rink. Both can be just as entertaining as that newly released movie. Catch the movie the next time.

Do you remember the Richard Simmons videos from back in the day? One thing I couldn't help but notice about him was how he had an eccentric, flamboyant, and energetic personality. I mean, how could you not see it? Simmons used his energetic and motivational demeanor to encourage people to lose weight and his high energy level always came through in those videos. He made exercising fun for people!

While I'm not saying you need to go out and try to get a Richard Simmons DVD, you do need to make your workouts fun. Strive for at least thirty minutes of moderate-intensity activity five days a week. Commit to the 150-minute minimum per week. If you can fit in more that's great. The more the better!

Your body does need to rest and recover, however, so don't overdo it. Go at a pace that works for you and listen to your body. It is important that you love your workout, and that exercise doesn't become a chore for you, or something that you grow to hate. If it is, you will do it for only a short time.

Remember, consistency is what we want. When you incorporate an enjoyable exercise plan into your routine, you will also notice a difference in how you feel and you'll be excited to see yourself more toned and possibly shedding some of those extra pounds.

I'll share a story with you about how I got into a fitness slump after having my daughter, Teya. I used to train three to five times a week in Tae Kwon Do and I planned to get back into it after the pregnancy. Circumstances changed and moving half-way across the country for a new job complicated getting back into a regular workout routine. I was in a state with no family, which meant no coverage for (or breaks from) the kids.

My work schedule got more hectic and demanding. I was tired. I noticed that I wasn't really gaining much weight due to the lack of exercise, but I also wasn't in shape either. I hated that. I would tell myself that I needed to get back into working out, but I lacked the follow through, making excuse after excuse. Missed workouts after missed workouts snowballed and then suddenly, I noticed that my jeans started to fit a little bit snugger.

That was the wakeup call for me to make a comeback. I mentally committed to changing my schedule and fitting workouts into the mix. No longer was I going to sit there with the formerly fit. I had gone off track and now it became time to get off the sideline and back into the game. The trick was to again make it exciting and entertaining.

One of the struggles for me during that time was being able to leave home to go workout. While I had plans to join a gym, my circumstances made it tough for me to do that. So, I modified my plan. We all know you don't need a gym to get in exercise. I ditched the gym and bought some workout DVDs and used them in my home theater. My daughters and my mom even joined me at times. It was fun!

First, you need to commit yourself to exercise. If you are not a physically active person, start off slow. Commit to five to ten minutes of exercise initially. Always consult your physician before engaging in a new exercise program. I want you healthy. Be sure your doctor is on board with your plans. Physical fitness should help tune your engine, not put extra stress on it. You can mix it up too. Some days you might work out in the afternoon, some days at lunch, and some in the morning.

Figure out what makes sense for you. Having a workout buddy also makes it enjoyable. You don't want to get bored doing the same types of exercises, so trying new moves will also help keep you motivated and will challenge you and your body. Downloading fitness or workout apps or hiring a personal trainer will also help with getting that exercise into your regular routine.

Rule #6: Manage your stress level.

Stress is a part of life, which creeps up on us even more during periods of uncertainty and life event changes. Our bodies and minds respond differently when faced with this kind of tension. Key to being successful is being able to get control of stress early on. Be sure to get help for what stresses are present in your life.

Money, jobs, and relationships are three main areas for stress. If your financial situation is worrying you, then take control of it now. Some people have good jobs but don't love the field they are in. They are afraid of being stuck in an unhappy predicament but aren't ready to give up a steady paycheck.

Stress is one of the contributors of high blood pressure. Years ago, my blood pressure was 145/110. I was constantly wiped out and often took naps after work and on the weekends. I could not show up with my A-game because I was exhausted.

I talked to my doctor about my blood pressure. We looked at all the factors contributing to high blood pressure: sodium intake, physical inactivity, alcohol consumption, and others. None of these were problematic for me. I worked out four to five times a week, never added salt to my foods, and always ate healthy. There was one factor remaining that we determined was driving my high blood pressure: *stress.*

That was it. I was so stressed out that it was negatively affecting my health. I ended up quitting my job and taking a new position. The stress level decreased and my blood pressure returned to normal levels.

Our bodies respond to stress in different ways and you need to understand how stress affects you. Additionally, what might be stressful to you, is not stressful to someone else. For me, my blood pressure spiked when I was stressed. Once you know how stress affects you, then you can identify habits to reduce it.

Embracing uncertainty means you will be living with change. Since stress is our response to change, you may experience varying levels of stress as you venture into unfamiliar territory on your field. It's okay for stress to exist, the key is to manage it so that you stay healthy. If you are feeling stressed, pay special attention to Chapter 19, "Control the 'S' Factor."

Rule #7: Avoid excessive wear and tear.

There is one element of your life that is with you to stay always: your body. Lovers come and go. Careers change. Children grow up and leave. Parents pass. The one life-long relationship you have is the one you have with your own body. Nurture it.

You treat your car with respect because you want to maintain its value and usefulness over a long period. You avoid extreme start-and-stop driving, excessive speeds, and towing more weight than recommended in your vehicle's owner's manual. You do these things so you can hang on to that car for quite some time and when that car has had enough, you replace it. You can't do the same thing with your body.

You get one and it can only take so much abuse and overuse. Be a little more compassionate for your body. Treat it with a little more tenderness. Getting proper nutrition, as previously discussed, is important. Making sure you are consuming the right vitamins is important too. For example, shooting for 200mg of Vitamin C in your daily intake can help ward off health issues like heart disease, stroke, and cancer. I'm not a medical expert and so I'm not going to give you specific other advice here, but you need to pay attention to how you are taking care of your body and not put too much unnecessary wear and tear on it.

A common theme you have heard me harp on is that you are here to play the long game and live a life of excellence. You are not here to set yourself up for continual exhaustion. It's imperative for you to focus on your health, your mental well-being, and to put yourself first.

Life throws at us countless obligations. While everyone lives under different circumstances, we possess a common responsibility—to first take care of ourselves. Maintaining YOU is your responsibility and it's not selfish. As with a car, take a time out for a personal check up. Look, feel, and be at your best by making smart decisions regarding your diet and nutrition. Live a healthy lifestyle, get enough sleep, reduce the stress in your life, and take a time out when needed. Don't neglect to tune your engine. You need it running at its peak for you to best serve others and to also get you to your destination.

COACH'S CHALKBOARD

1. Always make your health a priority.

2. Taking care of your well-being isn't selfish.

3. Check your numbers often.

4. Don't ignore health warning signs.

5. Make sure you are at your best so you can also best serve others.

CHAPTER 11:
SHOW UP

*"Success isn't always about greatness. It is about
consistency. Consistent hard work leads to success."*
—Dwayne "The Rock" Johnson

Early mornings with no crowds and empty bleachers. The lights are off and no one is around. That is where champions are made. It's not in a stadium on game day with thousands or tens of thousands of people watching and cheering them on. It's behind the scenes, with no one present, no cameras, and no applause, just pure work, grind, and hustle. That is the life of being in the top one percent—those elite players live it day in and day out. Many people never understand and appreciate the extent of the hard work required to be amongst the best.

Most do, though, realize that playing life's game is tough. When navigating through the day-to-day, to be successful there are times you need to be a fast-mover and a hard-hitter. The same is true in football and other competitive sports. Whichever "field" you are playing on, one important rule always holds true: *Nothing will go according to plan.* This is something I emphasized earlier in the book as well.

Life will push back on you, just as the defense tries to limit progress on the football field. Regardless of what gets thrown in your path, you just can't stop playing your game. Especially if this goal really matters to you. When life's challenges beat you down, you still have to keep showing up, be consistent, and continue to press onward. *Fall down seven times, stand up eight, remember?* That's how the saying goes.

Remember that anyone who is elite at their craft and successful got there because they weren't afraid to push their boundaries of comfortability and test their limits. They possessed the courage to try new things that didn't always work out. They always focused on being that 1% better and in doing so, they showed up to each day, pushed themselves harder, took risks, and did things that others would shy away from doing.

> " Winning doesn't just happen by coincidence. You have to grind. It's about the early mornings, late nights, overcoming adversity, and sacrificing more than you ever imagined you could. You have to love every second of the work no one ever sees."—Ryan Clark

This holds true whether someone is a professional athlete and playing at the highest level of their sport or being a successful business leader or entrepreneur. We've all taken risks and we've all fallen. As another saying goes, *a champion isn't defined by their wins, but how they can recover after they fall.*

Throughout this book, I've shared different parts of my journey in my career and with the Move the Ball movement. I never thought I would've ended up on the path I was on with Move the Ball which has led to incredible consulting work, speaking engagements, and getting to work with elite athletes, and as I've mentioned before, it was because I had the courage to keep showing up to each day, no matter what.

Even when faced with rejection, people blowing off meetings and not being respectful of my time, or others just flat out not seeing my value or my worth. I still showed up, ready to put in the work, and that's what you need to do too. When you show up consistently, you will get to where you want to go. It might not be as fast as you want it to be, but remember to trust the process and the results will come. These rules will help you to continue to show up on a daily basis.

Rule #1: Be obsessed with winning.

Great coaches and great athletes are obsessed with winning. They possess the motivation and the drive to stay focused and continually move forward in any situation, even when the outlook seems unclear. It's this winning attitude that gives them an edge. Besides having a yes-I-can-do attitude, they're ambitiously fired up and embrace uncertainty. They are comfortable with unknowns and use their go-getting, high-energy level to keep driving forward toward their goals.

These players possess a quality called *ambition with attitude*. This is what the "A" stands for in the MAD PRIDE acronym. *Ambition with Attitude* is an extra spunk that keeps successful people going, no matter what challenges they may face on their path. They believe in themselves and make winning a priority, today. They don't put off their goals until tomorrow. Today is their day and they take actions that will get them closer to the goal line. They make sure to win every day.

As the head coach of the Green Bay Packers, Vince Lombardi was known for not only wanting to win, but wanting to win now. Winning today was the only acceptable answer. His players were motivated by the fear of letting Coach Lombardi down. He pushed his players every day, both on and off the field. These athletes were fired up about winning. There was no other suitable outcome. Under Lombardi's leadership, the Packers won five NFL Championships in seven years, three of which were consecutive wins. The Packers became the first-ever Super Bowl champs in 1966 and then won Super Bowl II the following year. Lombardi's winning attitude has made him one of the most successful coaches in professional football history.

As you know, this behavior doesn't only exist in football. Let's take another example. Rudy Tomjanovich was a dynamic professional basketball head coach. During his first full season as head coach with the Houston Rockets, he guided the team to a Midwest Division title. During the next two seasons, Tomjanovich led the Rockets to back-to-back NBA championships. He was known for his leadership style and his intensity from the sideline. He had the heart of a champion and put tremendous pressure on himself and others to prepare for each game. Talented athletes like Scottie Pippen and Clyde Drexler were attracted to Tomjanovich's coaching style and successfully requested trades to play for the Houston Rockets. This coach truly possessed ambition with attitude and it showed. Tomjanovich also coached the U.S. men's national basketball team during the 2000 Olympic Games in Sydney, Australia. Under his direction, the U.S. team won the gold medal.

> In the world there are believers and then there are non-believers. For all of you non-believers out there, I have something to say to you... never underestimate the heart of a champion."
> —Rudy Tomjanovich

No matter what game you are playing, thriving in life requires playing your game with heart. Go in full-force and don't stop until you have crossed that goal line. As discussed earlier in this book, winning requires you to believe in yourself. Don't underestimate the power of your mental and emotional being. It's essential. Elite athletes are gifted; that's a given. So are successful business leaders and individuals. They also share another common skill: *the will to win.* Their desire to overcome any obstacle, climb any mountain, and weather through any storm is insurmountable. They *want* to win and won't stop until they have crossed the goal line. You are talented and you can do whatever you set out to do. You just need to be committed, be all-in and obsessed with winning, and then show up the right way each day.

Rule #2: The odds don't matter.

If I were to ask you to think of a time where a sports team was the underdog and somehow, someway managed to pull off an upset, you probably have a favorite that comes to mind. Then if I were to ask you to pick five more, you might need a minute or two, but surely you could come up with that list too. That's because it isn't uncommon for upsets to happen in sports and it's what gives fans hope that their team (while considered an underdog in a match-up) could pull off a victory. When the number one ranked team plays the lowest ranked team, fans still show up to cheer their team on, and guess what, the players of that underdog team still show up ready to play their heart out and try to get the W. They don't pay attention to the odds or listen to the noise, they stay locked in on what they need to in order to perform when it matters.

I'll share two examples of this that come to mind. During the 2021 college football season, Stanford faced the #3 ranked team Oregon. ESPN's Win Probability Model showed that Stanford had a 0.1% chance to beat Oregon with 1:51 left in the game. The odds didn't look good. But remember we shouldn't pay attention to that and neither did Coach Shaw or the Stanford football team. The Stanford Cardinal ended up tying the game in the 4th quarter and scored a touchdown in overtime to get the win. This victory meant that Stanford had won four straight games over Associated Press Top-3 teams, the longest active streak in FBS.

The other example I wanted to share was during the 2022 March Madness Tournament. During that tournament, St. Peter's University, a small Jesuit school in Jersey City, New Jersey was the 15th seed in the East Region. Usually, teams ranked that low don't make it that far in the tournament, but St. Peter's was about to show basketball fans everywhere that they shouldn't be counted out as they were about to go on what some would consider an "improbable run."

First, the Peacocks arguably had the most impressive opening victory in the tourney beating out No. 2 seed Kentucky during overtime with a final score of 85-79. This victory gave Kentucky Head Coach John Calipari arguably his worst loss ever in the NCAA tournament. St. Peter's was slated as an 18.5-point underdog in that game.

St. Peter's then punched its ticket to the Sweet 16 with a 70-60 takedown of No. 7 seed Murray State in the second round, making them just the third No. 15 seed in tournament history to advance into the Sweet 16. If you're a college basketball fan, you might recall that Oral Roberts busted tournament brackets in a similar fashion the year before.

But wait, St. Peter's wasn't done just yet. Only 0.87% of March Madness brackets had St. Peter's chosen to make it to the Elite Eight. To do so, the Peacocks would have to face No. 3 seed Purdue's Boilermakers. They continued with their historic Cinderella story adding Purdue to their string of March Madness upsets, winning 67-64. They ended up facing North Carolina in the next round and didn't quite pull off the win, but the team still had so much to be proud of being the first No. 15 seed in NCAA tournament history to ever make it to the Elite Eight. Additionally, St. Peter's was the first Metro Atlantic Athletic Conference (MAAC) team to ever win three March

Madness games.

While these are two feel good stories with sports teams, this principle of not paying attention to the odds extends beyond a football field or a basketball court into real life. As a personal example, I was a single parent at 18 years old. According to the National Conference of State Legislatures, less than two percent of teen moms finish college by age 30. Not a high number, is it? Do you think this was something that I paid attention to or was going to let stop me? Of course not. With the support of my parents, I knuckled down, showed up, and completed two engineering degrees in 4½ years. Take those statistics!

The thing about whatever "odds" you might be facing is that thing is just a number. When things seem stacked against you, that just means that you will need to work harder to get to where you want to go, but that doesn't mean that the goal or the dream is impossible. As discussed throughout this book, you just need to figure out your game plan and execute on it. Show up and do what you need to, the odds don't matter.

Rule #3: Play each day with intention.

All of us have the same amount of time each day, no more and no less. But it's what you do with that time that will determine whether you are moving forward or backwards in life. This principle of showing up requires you to be a person of your vision and to focus on what matters instead of getting caught up in the day-to-day and living in a reactionary mode. You need to approach each day with purpose and intention instead of just trying to survive and make it to another day.

In several chapters of this book, I have highlighted the need to develop effective habits, to plan out your days and your weeks, and how to manage your time and your mindset to be productive. Over the years, a common comment I get from clients is that they don't have a lot of free time because of work or family commitments, and so they feel stuck and are looking for help. Keep in mind that we all have different work and personal obligations. It's a matter of prioritizing our time each week, both work and "free time."

In the work context, are you spending your time on the tasks that really matter, or are you bogged down with processes and meetings that don't add value? If the latter is the case, I would challenge you to have the conversation with your leadership and identify solutions to make the work tasks more efficient for you and everyone on the team. When it comes to your time outside of work, it comes down to your choices. How much time are you wasting on social media? How much television or Netflix do you watch? There's nothing wrong with having some entertainment but ask yourself are you being excessive with it. Examine what you are spending your time on and if those activities are serving you and your goals.

Another very important point to make here is that all of us are going to have different commitments and so the amount of "free time" that a single person with no kids has will likely be different than a married couple with four children at home. You have to look at the time that you have available for you outside of your family and job obligations and make sure you are being selective with how you spend your time. Don't compare your situation to someone else's and what their calendar might look like.

Rule #4: Elevation requires separation.

Showing up in life the right way means eliminating what does not help you evolve. It's about hanging around people you want to be influenced by. It's about chasing dreams not approval. It's about being unapologetically you. That sounds good, doesn't it? But what am I really getting at here?

First, you need to ditch those habits that aren't productive. There's a whole chapter you read that went into depth on that. Tying this back to Rule #3, it's eliminating those tasks and activities that are not helping you achieve your business, career, and personal goals. Next, it means surrounding yourself with the right people that will help you to reach that next level.

I would challenge you, as mentioned in "Get Inside the Huddle," to look at who are you spending your time with. Are they the right people for where you want to go next? The key here is *your future success*. Sometimes we need to change up our circle for that next chapter. When I left corporate America to become an entrepreneur, I completely changed my circle. That didn't mean that I stopped being friends with people from my corporate life, but the people I spent the majority of my time with were entrepreneurs. The world of entrepreneurship is a very different environment and I wanted to learn and grow from people who had walked in the shoes that I had decided to step into.

Importantly, you also need to separate yourself from those experiences in your past that are holding you back. Something that I discuss often on my *Move the Ball* podcast with my NFL guests is the importance of focusing on the next play and forgetting the last one. Too often, people become stuck because they are hanging onto a failed relationship, business outcome, or experience, and it is preventing them from moving on. If you're someone who is holding onto something in your past or using that as an excuse, it's time to let that go.

Lastly, elevation requires separation from the noise, the haters, and the doubters out there. "With or Without You" will go into more detail on this, but the sooner you can mentally condition yourself to tune all of that out, the easier it will be for you to show up and handle what you need to each day.

As an example, the University of Alabama football team is an organization that has a lot of press around it because of it being a storied college football program. From coaching greats like Paul "Bear" Bryant to Nick Saban, Alabama football knows how to win. For Alabama, the 2020 National Championship was their 18th claimed National title and their sixth since Nick Saban took over the program in 2007. During the 2021 season, the team was looking to add some more accomplishments to their list, with fans and haters eagerly watching to see what would take place that year.

Jalyn Armour-Davis, an NFL defensive back who was drafted in the 4th round of the 2022 NFL Draft by the Baltimore Ravens, was on that 2021 Alabama team. He joined me on Season 3 of my *Move the Ball* podcast where we discussed the 2021 season and how Alabama was able to beat out the #1 ranked Georgia Bulldogs to win the 2021 SEC Championship. This is part of what Jalyn said:

> *"It was a lot of talking, a lot of doubt. And you know, around us as a team throughout the season, we had a lot of ups and downs, a lot of close, tough games. Even before the season, everyone is you know, it's Alabama's down year and all of that. And the entire year, even when we had great games, we were always out to prove people wrong because everyone still had doubts about us...We weren't satisfied, but we knew it took that long, we opened up the people's eyes that were closed, that were sleeping on us. I think that game we really had to put our foot down and make a statement and we did."*

Highly competitive athletes like Jalyn are used to hearing praise one day and negative comments the next day, sometimes from the same people. It's part of the business of competitive sports combined with social media. These elite athletes are trained to tune out and separate themselves from the noise. Throughout life you are going to have people who are doubters and haters, the sooner you can get those people out of your head, the better.

Rule #5: Be where your feet are.

"Be where your feet are" is a common saying in football. What this means is being fully present in the moment and staying locked in on the business you are trying to handle in that moment. Life is going to come at you fast, and you can only control the things you can control, so you need to stay focused on those things so you can continue to go forward.

Being fully present also requires you to be mindful of and to protect your energy. If you don't separate yourself from your distractions, your distractions will separate you from your goals and the life you want. Be aware of how you are spending not just your time, but also where you are spending your energy.

Rule #6: Always do it first class.

No matter what it is you are looking to accomplish in business, your career, or your life, anything you do, you should do it *first class*. After all, you are a professional and should be focused on excellence. Notice I did say excellence, not perfection.

Someone who knows all about excellence and a first-class mentality is retired NFL tight end and back-to-back Super Bowl champion Byron Chamberlain. Byron is a dear friend and colleague and someone who I've had on my *Move the Ball* podcast on multiple occasions. The first time I had him on the show we discussed several topics, including the importance of earning the respect of your peers, finding an invested mentor, what it's like winning back-to-back championships, and why he's committed to doing everything "first class."

Byron shared his experience getting drafted by the Denver Broncos, and on his very first day in the Broncos building with then head coach Mike Shanahan, Coach Shahan told the team they were going to do things one way there and one way only. That it was going to be first class and that was going to be in everything the team did, from the way they dressed, to the way they practiced, to the way they ate, and to the way they played. It was going to be first class or not at all. Byron shared that those words had always stuck with him and he has applied them to everything he has done both in football and in life, never settling for mediocrity. Anything he does he's going to give it his all and give it his best.

This is the same way you need to approach anything you are doing, always first class. Throughout my career in corporate and as an entrepreneur, I've always been one of those people who has had the courage to push through challenges, not listened to the doubters, and also strove for excellence in everything that I did. The thing about that too is other people will see that you hold yourself to that kind of standard and opportunities will come your way because you approach all your dealings and your life with this first-class standard.

Rule #7: This isn't just about you.

While I wrote this book because I wanted to help you become the best version of yourself, I also want you to remember that it's not just about you. If you've listened to my *Move the Ball* podcast or heard me speak on a stage or train during a workshop, you know that something else I emphasize is that moving the ball is not just about what you accomplish in life, but it's also about what you inspire others to do as well.

People are always watching you and you never know who you are motivating. When you show up for yourself, you show up for others too. You teach them that despite all the setbacks, all the heartbreaks, and all the losses, you get stronger and that it can make them stronger too. You give them hope, enable them to believe in themselves, empower them to be bold, and demonstrate to them that when they show up ready to play their game, they too can accomplish their goals.

Now I want to challenge you to consider how you are approaching and handling each day. Are you giving enough to each day and are you doing enough? How are you showing up on the days you aren't feeling motivated? Are you still bringing that commitment and discipline on those days?

I was in Tampa at a dinner meeting with a friend, Ricky Sailor, who is a sports agent and brand manager, and we were talking about competitive athletes. He said the reason why athletes make good workers is because they show up, even on the days they don't want to. They are conditioned to perform, even when they aren't feeling 100% or don't want to be at practice. They are there, ready to work. It was that conversation that actually gave me the idea to write this book about how you need to show up to life. It truly is the difference maker between those that live the life they want and those who live a life with regret. Make sure you are being fully present and not just going through the motions.

Your intention coupled with your action creates your reality. A mentality centered around excellence focuses you on being the best you can be and bringing that version of yourself forward each day. An obsession with winning keeps you going in the face of adversity and obstacles. We've got to show up because of and despite the struggles. When we do this, we may be tired, feel weak, and even battered at times, but the satisfaction of pushing through will feel amazing and give you more motivation to tackle the next challenge. Remember too, give yourself as many chances as you need to get it right and get across the goal line. Failures and setbacks are part of the process. There is no need to keep score either. Don't let negative emotions or experiences hold you hostage, just keep learning, keep going, and keep showing up.

COACH'S CHALKBOARD

1. The vision is easy, it's the doing that separates the winners from the losers.

2. If it were easy, everyone would do it.

3. Commit to consistency.

4. Keep showing up when most people would quit.

5. Put your focus on today. Yesterday is over with and tomorrow doesn't matter yet.

6. Show up to every moment like you belong there.

7. Whatever you do, always do it first class.

CHAPTER 12:
THE ONE PERCENT

*"The only competition that matters is the one that takes
place within yourself."*
—Pete Carroll

Most people won't ever understand the work required to be elite. They won't grasp why great athletes wake up two hours before the sunrise to go jogging around the neighborhood or why they are still on the field working on drills long after everyone else has gone home. They won't get why athletes do pushups during commercial breaks and are so meticulous about what they put in their bodies. These same people won't understand why a player shows up early to a workout, stresses over ten more pounds on a bench press, or gets so hyped up over one more rep. They won't understand why these high performers sprint through agility ladders, race around cones, and flip tires, all trying to shave five-hundredths of a second off their time.

The one-percent mentality is what the other ninety-plus percent won't ever fully comprehend. You see, majority of people in the world don't have the desire or the discipline to show up to life and put the work in that is required to live a life of excellence.

Achieving greatness requires a relentless work ethic. It means making moves every single day. It means using and strengthening your muscles on a consistent basis, physical ones as an athlete or fitness junkie, or mental ones as a player wanting to excel in business and in life.

To reach greatness, there can be no days off (yes you can call a timeout and take a day for rest and recovery, that is different as that is still a strategic part of your plan for being able to move the ball). It's important to note that even if you are taking a period to recover, that doesn't mean you aren't engaged in other activities that are helping you to level up and become better.

The 1% athlete is always looking at how they can improve and the desire to do so is unwavering. For these individuals, like everyone else, there will be days they feel like they are going backwards instead of forwards. There will be days where mistakes are made, where they drop or fumble the ball, or where they fail. There will be "bad" days. They experience days where it seems like everyone, and everything, are against them. But no matter what, there will be *no* day that they give up. There will be *no* day that they give in or that they concede defeat. They will keep striving for victory and they will keep fighting the battles they need to along the way.

The 1% player keeps on playing the game, no matter what. As long as the goals remain valid, they keep striving to achieve them. No excuses, period. Maximum commitment to the goal. 100% focus. They just embrace the suck that comes along the way and they keep on moving. They seek out discomfort, look for the difficult tasks, step up for challenges, and do a little extra every single day. That's how the one percent train for greatness.

To train like a great athlete, and be in the top percent, you must first be committed to winning. You must *want it* enough. "Own Your Game" stressed the importance of ownership and your personal commitment. To win in life, your inner spark must be charged and ready to detonate. Accomplished winners find the mental, physical, and emotional strength to persevere through adverse situations. So should you. They refuse to be in the ninety percent of people who give up when things get tough and strive to be in the small number who actually make their dreams a reality.

The 1% player, as a competitor and a leader, always maintains a focus on continual improvement. While all the elements of MAD PRIDE are characteristics exhibited by this type of individual, two worth calling out here are the "P" which stands for *Practice with Purpose*, and the "I" which stands for *Improvement Focused*.

Practice, and doing it with a specific purpose, is an essential part of winning. Whether you are playing sports or the game of life, you cannot underestimate the importance of practice. In his best-selling book, *Outliers: The Story of Success*, author Malcom Gladwell talks about the need to practice. He discusses the "10,000-hour rule" which he claimed was the amount of practice that was required to ace a skill. Hey, no one said mastery would be easy. Greatness doesn't happen overnight and no player is a superstar without practice. They're always working on some aspect of their game and are intentional about how they practice.

At 6'6" and 255 pounds, NFL tight end Tyler Eifert is a big guy. Eifert, who was a first-round draft pick (21st overall) by the Cincinnati Bengals in the 2013 NFL Draft was no stranger to practice. When Eifert was a student at Bishop Dwenger High School in Fort Wayne, Indiana, he didn't think he was good enough to play college football. His solution: practice with purpose.

Eifert worked on the areas he needed to in order to become a high performing football player. As a high school senior, he played both the tight end and defensive back positions. That year he scored nine touchdowns, had ninety-seven tackles, and recorded five interceptions. He then went on to play college football at Notre Dame. During the Fighting Irish's perfect season in 2012, he caught fifty passes for 685 yards and four touchdowns. That year he also won the prestigious John Mackey Award, which is presented to the most outstanding college tight end. Eifert was also named second team All-

American by the *Associated Press* in 2012. Eifert's success continued in the NFL where, during his career, he had 220+ receptions, 2,500+ receiving yards, 25+ touchdowns, and he was a Pro-Bowler in 2015.

> " *In my junior year during basketball season, I was up at 4:30 a.m. driving to work out for football..."—Tyler Eifert told Sports Illustrated*

One huge mistake many athletes and individuals make in life is assuming that they are *good enough*. Then they feel entitled and are disgruntled when what they want in life is not handed to them. Winning life's game involves active participation. You don't win by being a spectator and you will not achieve your goals without continuous improvement. "Ditch the Old Clothes in the Locker Room" highlighted the need to change your habits. If you want to be successful in the future, you cannot use the same practices that got you where you are today. You must make changes immediately— adopt new behaviors and execute different plays.

Self-awareness is an important part of planning your next moves. You must be aware of what is and what is not currently working for you. What is prohibiting you from moving forward? Where can you improve? If you haven't done this previously, make sure you carve out some time and examine this.

One elite NFL player who has trained and gone hard throughout his entire football career is NFL running back Derrick Henry. A beast on the field, Henry's competitive spirit has been with him his entire life. In high school, as a five-star recruit, he set the national high school record for career rushing yards with 12,124 yards. During his junior season in college, playing for the Alabama Crimson Tide, Henry broke Herschel Walker's Southeastern Conference (SEC) single season rushing attempts record with 395 rushing attempts. Henry also won the 2015 Heisman Trophy, the Doak Walker Award, the Maxwell Award, the Walter Camp Award, and was an integral part of Alabama's football team in 2015 when they won the College Football Playoff (CFP) National Championship against Clemson on January 11, 2016.

Henry was drafted in the second round of the 2016 NFL Draft by the Tennessee Titans. He then led the league in rushing yards for the 2019 season as well as rushing touchdowns (tied with Green Bay Packers running back Aaron Jones). In 2020, Henry again led the NFL in rushing yards and touchdowns and became the eighth player in NFL history to rush for over 2,000 yards in a single season (the last person to achieve this was Adrian Peterson in 2012 with the Minnesota Vikings). Henry also won the Associated Press NFL Offensive Player of the Year Award in 2020.

It is without question that Derrick Henry is among the best of the best. There are many reasons why he is the elite of the elite. On the field he has excellent eyes, strong arms, good quickness, and can get into spaces quickly and make the right cuts. He keeps his legs churning even when a defensive player makes an initial hit and according to Pro Football Focus, he led the NFL by picking up an average of 4.2 yards after contact in the regular season, and that number increased to 4.7 yards per carry in the playoffs. Henry can also turn on the afterburners and has reached top speed of over 21 miles per hour during explosive runs down the field.

Derrick Henry is the only NFL player to have achieved single season rushing yards of 2,000+ yards in high school, in college, and in the NFL

Henry was built different. There's no doubt he has established himself as one of the biggest skill players in the NFL. At 6 foot 3 and 247 pounds, it isn't just about his size though. Another thing that has led to his incredible success is him being *improvement focused,* the "I" in MAD PRIDE. He is always looking at how he can build muscle on top of muscle and keep his body in top shape. He refrains from getting complacent like many players when they reach success; he keeps pushing himself to achieve more.

Take NFL Wide Receiver and 2019 CFP National Champion, Ja'Marr Chase, as another example. During his rookie season, Ja'Marr had an incredible year in the NFL with 1,455 receiving yards and 13 receiving touchdowns. He won the 2021 NFL AP Offensive Rookie of the Year Award (becoming the first wide receiver to win the award since Odell Beckham Jr. in 2014). Ja'Marr was also instrumental in the Bengals getting to Super Bowl LVI.

While the list of accolades could go on and on, what makes Ja'Marr a top athlete is he isn't satisfied with these accomplishments; he's always striving for more. When Ja'Marr and I talked the summer before the 2022 NFL season, he was determined to break every record with the Cincinnati Bengals. What I will say is Ja'Marr is definitely one of those people who will put in that work to achieve his goals. He's a high performer who won't get complacent and is never satisfied. He always pushes himself to do and be better.

The takeaway here is that the great athletes maintain a 100% focus on continuous improvement. They look at how they can continue to get just one percent better every day. This mentality is essential to winning in sports and in life. It starts with a mindset that incorporates continuous improvement into your regimen. This applies to whatever you are looking to do in life, whether it be personal, business, or career goals.

Very early in my career I wasn't always successful at getting people to do what I wanted. I knew I needed to improve my influencing skills. It was easier for me to sway co-workers who would follow me anywhere. It was a different game when they wouldn't. I spent time understanding other techniques and approaches to influencing. I read books on the subject and even attended a short class. I learned how to conduct difficult conversations with people and continually practiced the new tools I had learned. My success was determined by how I approached people. By applying a different set of skills, I was able to yield the results I desired. If I wasn't willing to invest in my self-improvement, the outcome would have been different.

Often times, I hear people talking about how they want a promotion. Afterall, a promotion usually comes with more money. Who wouldn't want that, right?

The problem with some who approach me on this topic is they have failed to think critically about if they are ready for that promotion. On the surface, they believe they are ready. However, if they did an in-depth assessment, their view might be different. If you are considering going after a promotion and you think you are ready for a new role with more responsibility, here are some questions you can ask yourself to see where you might stand:

- *What do I need to know to position me for my next job?*

- *What experiences make me ready to move to the next level?*

- *Have I mastered the skills that I need?*

- *If not, how can I use my current job to acquire these skills? Are there any opportunities outside of work for self-development?*

- *Am I ready to take the risks expected of me with a promotion?*

If after this deeper look you are ready, congratulations. The next step is to map out your plan to get that new promotion. If it's not time yet, I applaud you for being honest with yourself. Succeeding in life starts with self-awareness and then having an improvement focus. Now you must make the commitment to self-development. Review your answers to the above questions and identify what specific improvements are needed in your life. Next, put that playbook together and start working on that one percent daily improvement in these areas. Think creatively and stretch beyond your comfort zone. Then execute your plan. Don't settle for who you are today, focus on obtaining new skills or strengthening current ones and you will make progress towards your goals.

One other important point to mention here is the 1% player also isn't concerned with the competition, per se. They aren't focused on playing the game better than any one individual, but rather are consumed with striving to be better than the person they were yesterday. They are always looking to outwork that version of who they were the day before. That is their ultimate goal: *me vs. me.* They don't worry about what others are doing and don't get distracted by that noise. They also don't break promises to themselves, meaning if they say they're going to do something, they go do it. They focus on what they're going after, and they take action to follow through on that.

Many qualities separate the 1% athletes and leaders in life from the good, the bad, and the mediocre. Pushing boundaries, dealing with uncertainty, and training for greatness can be challenging and stressful. Succeeding in this realm requires going hard—mentally, physically, and emotionally. Sometimes it takes doing something you've never done before if you want to get to a place that you've never been.

The harder you train, the harder you'll be to beat. You'll be able to effectively move through the unknowns, the uncomfortable times, and the adversity. You will also be able to create your own opportunities for excellence. It all begins when you train for greatness. So, lace up your cleats, play like an elite athlete, and crush each day by committing to winning, dedicating time for self-improvement, becoming one percent better each day, and always practicing your craft with purpose. It starts with you, so make the commitment right now to change up the game, to show up, and to be in the one percent. Your grind may go unnoticed but, trust me, when you do these things, your results won't.

COACH'S CHALKBOARD

1. To be in the 1%, you must do what the other 99% won't do.

2. Being in the 1% requires you to have a relentless work ethic coupled with an unwavering determination.

3. Show up each day and make moves happen. No excuses.

4. If you want to be great, there are no days off.

5. The 1% are not complacent and have dedicated their lives to continuous self-improvement.

6. Elite athletes practice with purpose and are intentional on what skills they work on.

7. Outwork yesterday and get 1% better each day.

CHAPTER 13:
ALL LOCKED IN

*"The most important key to achieving great success is to
decide upon your goal, and launch,
get started, take action, move."*
—John Wooden

Tom Brady. It's a name football fans either love to hear or one that they hate. But no matter which side you fall on, Tom Brady must be given credit here: He is a GOAT. Not only is Tom an example of one of the best-of-the-best athletes, but his incredible story also serves as a reminder to all of us that your past does not define who you can become.

Let's look back at Brady's college football career. When Michigan and Nebraska split the college football national championship title in 1997, Brady was a quarterback for the University of Michigan. However, he was not the starting quarterback. In fact, he was far from it. Brian Griese was the starter who had led the Wolverines that year setting Michigan single season records with 193 pass completions and 307 pass attempts. During Michigan's Rose Bowl victory against Washington State (the game that positioned Michigan to become the national champs), it was Brian Griese that was named game MVP, having completed 18 of 30 passes for 251 yards and three touchdowns.

What about Tom? Where was he? Was he the next quarterback in line? Nope.

At one point, Tom was the seventh-string quarterback on Michigan's roster. He eventually moved up to third string, but he was still worried he wouldn't get a chance to pass the two quarterbacks ahead of him on the depth chart. In 1998, when Brady had the opportunity to be a starter, he still battled Drew Henson, a younger, athletically gifted quarterback for the #1 spot. Brady eventually became the full-time starting quarterback that season, throwing for 2,427 yards, fourteen touchdowns, and ten interceptions. As the starting quarterback his senior year, Brady passed for 2,217 yards, completed 61% of his passes, and finished the season with sixteen touchdowns and six interceptions. His win-loss record as a starting quarterback was 20-5 and Brady finished his career with the Michigan Wolverines ranking third in school history with 710 attempts and 442 completions. Brady also ranked in the top five in passing yards at Michigan with 5,351 yards and a pass completion rate of 62.3% in his career.

During the 2000 NFL Draft, Brady was selected in the sixth round as the 199th pick by the New England Patriots. Both Brady and his family thought he would be drafted in the second or third round and were stunned when six other quarterbacks were drafted before him.

Remember what I said about your past doesn't define who you can become? Even though Tom was a late-round NFL draft pick, it is without question that Brady's professional football career has been remarkable. At the time he got his first Super Bowl win, Brady (being 24 years and 6 months old) was the youngest quarterback to win such a championship by helping the Patriots beat the St. Louis Rams 20-17 in 2002. Throughout his career with the Patriots, Brady would go on to win four more Super Bowls, including a 28-3 comeback victory over the Atlanta Falcons in 2016. Then he would win another Super Bowl with the Tampa Bay Buccaneers at 43 years old, making him the oldest quarterback to win a Super Bowl. His amazing accomplishments over his 20+ years have made him one of the greatest quarterbacks of all time.

Now there are many different qualities about Tom Brady that make him a super elite athlete. But the one I want to highlight here is Brady's ability to remain mentally *locked in* and do what needs to be done to lead his team to a victory. That's the case whether he and his team are dominating a game from the get-go or they are in a crunch-time, comeback situation.

If you listen to professional athletes talk during press conferences or watch videos on YouTube or see posts on social media, they always discuss the need to remain locked in and to handle their business.

"All locked in" is something you'll often see them post. This is also a common theme that I've discussed with the pro athletes who have appeared on my *Move the Ball* podcast.

So, what exactly does it mean to be locked in? It means being fully attuned to or in synch with the game or the activity that you are engaged in, and as a result, play superbly and commit no mental errors. It means getting the job done and performing at whatever it is you set out to do with excellence. For example, a basketball player who shoots 6-for-6 from three-point distance is staying locked in, making the right shooting decisions, and hitting them with accuracy. A defensive back in football who is covering his player well and not letting his opponent make any catches or big plays is a defensive player who is on lock, meaning his on-the-field awareness is high and he is performing at optimum effectiveness.

Baseball players are said to be locked in when they swing only at strikes and hit every strike squarely (if they are hitters) or if they breeze through the opposing lineup with sharp control and the opponents manage no hard hits against them (if they are pitchers). From these examples you can see that this term applies to different types of performance in different sports, but it always implies great concentration and effectiveness by the locked-in player in whatever the game or event may be.

The game of life is no different. Putting in the grind is that "extra something" that separates the most successful people from the rest. We've already discussed throughout this book the importance of showing up each day with intention and with purpose. How you show up matters, you know this. But it isn't just about showing up with the right mindset and bringing the positive energy to each day. Those things are important, but it's the passion, perseverance, and stamina we must channel in order to stick with our dreams until they become a reality.

You get what you focus on in life, so it's important to remain locked in on the tasks and activities that you need accomplish. You have to focus on the possibilities for success, not on the potential for failure. To do this you must *nix the distractions* and *protect your focus*.

Rule #1: Feed your focus and starve your distractions.

When it comes to your goals, you need to stay the course if you want to move toward and get across the goal line. But in a world full of notifications and social media, it's extremely easy to lose focus. How do you refrain from the distractions? How do you not let the noise get in the way?

What this comes down to is learning to set boundaries and not compromising your principles. You've heard me say before that you are the quarterback and that you need to take ownership on your life's field. In "What Color is Your Jersey," it was discussed that you need to be clear on the "game" you're playing. Once you have that clarity, it's easier to figure out what your strategy should be and what actions you need to take to be able to be successful.

Being clear on your objective also makes it easier for you to set boundaries so you can spend your time doing the right activities and tasks that will help you make that forward progress. Part of that boundary setting is tuning out the things that are distracting you and consuming your time unnecessarily.

Take a minute and think about how often you look at your phone throughout the day because of a notification or an alert you receive. Every time that happens, your focus is being taken away from the task you were working on and now you have become distracted. That distraction might only be for a few seconds, but often what happens is now you are reacting and responding to whatever notification popped up and that's just the beginning. Writing a text message to someone, responding to a tweet, or commenting on a social media post then turns into a half an hour (or more) of engaging with people that had nothing to do with the original thing you were working on. Heaven forbid that whatever distracted you in the first place got you all riled up.

When this happens, that response could turn into hours of wasted efforts on something you shouldn't have paid attention to in the first place. Then you look at the clock and wonder where the time went! Remember what I said at the beginning of this book about how time flies? This is part of what I was referring to.

Part of what makes competitive athletes successful at their sport is the ability to not only remain disciplined but also locked in. You have to train like an athlete here and be very disciplined when it comes to your distractions. Starve them. Ignore those notifications. Turn off your notifications even. But it isn't only notifications on your phone that can be distractions. Those are just one type. Distractions can be in the form of negativity, self-doubt, fear, other people's opinions, and more. Take an inventory of what is currently interrupting you on a routine basis and preventing you from staying focused on the activities you need to be locked in on. Establish your boundaries and nix the distractions.

Rule #2: Protect your focus.

Eliminating distractions and protecting your focus go hand in hand to remaining all locked in. To do this, you must be selective with who and what you are giving your time to. This goes back to setting boundaries and saying "No" to the things that aren't serving a purpose for you each day. This is also easier said than done.

One reason why people struggle with this is they are uncomfortable with using the word "No." This is because people tend to have a negative connotation around this word. Therefore, they don't like to say no to people because they associate it with something negative. But really, what saying no allows you to do is to establish priorities and move you closer to achieving your goals and objectives. It allows you to qualify who and what you're going to spend your time on.

Saying no can also prevent others from taking advantage of you and your time. So, if someone always comes to you to take care of a task for them, let's say in the workplace, but it's not even within your scope of responsibility, that takes you away from another activity that you need to do, then that is a problem.

Maybe it's not even in the workplace, it can be outside of the job context. If you continually allow people to use your time to do other things, then that's counterproductive to what you need to be focused on. As an example, when you don't say no, you are actually being an enabler and helping people who need to help themselves. I'll explain.

Have you ever had someone who always comes to you for help with their problems? Because they're just looking for you to give them the answers, they're not looking to work through the things themselves. And so, if you say no to them, and that you're not going to give them the time, then that forces them to kind of figure their own stuff out. And if you say no enough, then they're not going to come to you anymore. They may go bother someone else. But maybe they'll figure it out themselves, too.

Whether someone is coming to you to fix their problems or to throw a work task over the wall to you or for some other reason, all of these things take time away from your day and detract you from your focus. You need to not let other people consume your time unless you're willing to give it to them. It's okay to give people your time, but you need to be aware of how much of it you are allowing them to use. You need to be disciplined and set boundaries so that you can protect your focus as well.

Here's another way to look at it. I got this from my good friend, JJ Birden, a former wide receiver who played college football at Oregon and went on to play nine seasons in the NFL. What JJ said to me was you have to protect your focus like it's a million-dollar suitcase. What he meant by that is if you had $1 million in a suitcase, you must think about how you would protect that suitcase as you're walking through the airport. In that scenario, you would be completely dialed in on protecting it because you knew what was inside it.

> *Protect your focus like it's a million-dollar suitcase." —JJ Birden*

Well, this is the same thing you need to do with your focus. You need to protect it because you would get so much more productivity in your day if you remained truly focused on the important activities you needed to complete each day. JJ likes to share this example, as do I, as it's a wonderful way to understand the importance of protecting your focus and the value that could be created if you remain locked in and undistracted. Become more aware of what's really worth your time and your energy.

Rule #3: Increase your level of non-acceptance.

It probably doesn't come as a surprise to you that I have spent a considerable amount of time studying professional athletes, coaches, high performance trainers, and great business leaders. Since I opened this chapter mentioning Tom Brady, I now want to share one of my favorite quotes from him.

> *"Too often in life, something happens, and we blame other people for us not being happy or satisfied or fulfilled. So, the point is, we all have choices, and we make the choice to accept people or situations or to not accept situations."*

I share this quote with you because we all have unpleasant outcomes and circumstances that occur in our life. That's what makes life interesting, frustrating, challenging, and sometimes exciting (usually after the fact, when we reflect on the situation). A crucial theme in this book has been that we always have choices. When it comes to showing up in life, you decide what kind of mindset you are going to bring to the day, what you are going to wear, what you are going to eat, what you are going to spend your time on, and so much more. Plenty of choices. One of those choices needs to be *to accept situations as they are or to not accept them and do something about it.*

A very successful entrepreneur and friend of mine, Brandon Steiner, and I also recently had a conversation around the topic of choosing not to accept situations as they are. To share a little about Brandon's background, Brandon is an author, speaker, media personality, and sports business icon who was the founder and CEO of Steiner Sports. Brandon also founded Athletes Direct and the CollectibleXchange, which is an open marketplace for athletes and fans that allows individuals to buy, sell, appraise, and authenticate all of their sports memorabilia and collectibles.

During our conversation he talked about how it's important that you become accountable, not based on the circumstances you are put in, but because you have the ability to change your circumstances. He continued to share that especially in the uncertain environment we were currently living in, that there's a lot of excuses being thrown around by people. As he said, "There's a lot of cheese and crackers to go with people's wine."

Brandon continued discussing that no matter what circumstances are presented to us, there is always room for an opportunity for those who are locked in to look at their circumstances, the adversity they may be facing, and to get up and do something about it. They don't just throw their hands up in the air or shrug their shoulders. Nope. They show up to life with their priorities on lock and figure out what opportunities they can create.

A point he wanted to make sure he emphasized during our chat was that you have to have a high-level of non-acceptance to be successful in life. This doesn't matter if you're ten years old or fifty. You need to have the courage to say, "I'm not putting up with *this*," whatever the "this" might be. You have to say that you have a non-tolerance for a situation and are going to do something about it.

When Brandon was ten years old, he had a non-tolerance for his situation about wearing the same clothes, the hand-me downs that he had, and so even at ten, he decided that he was going to go get a job. He made that happen even as a kid. He had made the choice to not accept the conditions as they existed and found a way to achieve his objective of putting himself in a situation where he didn't have to wear those old clothes.

Look at your current environment. If you don't feel like you are getting very far, is it because you have a low level of non-acceptance? Have you been willing to tolerate things that you shouldn't even though they aren't serving you?

If that is the case, make today the day that this all changes. Put your foot in the ground, get your lock on, and say "I'm not putting up with this anymore." This could be a relationship, a job, or something else.

Maybe it's the people in your circle. We discussed this in "Get Inside the Huddle." Maybe it's time to not want to be friends with the people who are dragging you down. This was an important concept discussed in my *Move the Ball* book, in the "Drop the Dead Weight" chapter. If you have a copy of *Move the Ball*, it might be worth re-reading if you are struggling with the people in your inner sphere. Now is the time to turn up the volume of your non-acceptance because, once you do, non-acceptance is like the entry point to dreaming big. Once you have made it a priority to get out of that situation, you can then really lock in on the right things to get you moving in the direction you want to go.

Once you have this non-acceptance you really start figuring out what you need to do to get out of your current situation and identifying the details of your game plan for a better life. This also helps you to dream about what you want your future state to be instead of settling for what it is. A lot of times people just succumb to their circumstances and just settle. They make excuses as to why something cannot happen. What you need to say, "You know what? I'm not going to stand for *this*." Stop making excuses and turn up your level of non-acceptance. The choice is always yours.

The greatest athletes and most successful people in life make the choice to get in the "zone" and remain "locked in" to be able to move the ball forward at all times. This is true when things are going well and when they are faced with times of adversity or challenge. To keep your priorities on lock, you need to block out all the distractions, protect your focus, silence any fears or doubts that might creep in, and then take daily action that will get you closer to the goal line. Remaining locked in will help ensure that you create the future that you want instead of enduring and settling for the future that you get.

COACH'S CHALKBOARD

1. If you want to win in life, you must be all locked in and be where your feet are.

2. Remaining focused is a competitive advantage.

3. Starve your distractions.

4. Protect your focus like it's a million-dollar suitcase.

5. Be unwilling to accept circumstances or situations that aren't positioning you for success.

CHAPTER 14:
TRUST THE PROCESS

*"There are two pains in life. There is the pain of discipline
and the pain of disappointment. If you can handle the pain of
discipline, then you'll never have to deal with the
pain of disappointment."*
—Nick Saban

College Station has been known as one of the best places to live in Texas. It is a town that offers their residents small-town charm, a dense suburban feel, a low cost of living, and let's not forget, there's college football too. Plenty of reasons to be there.

Then there was this one time on a fall night in College Station when over 100,000 fans poured into Kyle Stadium to see history being made. These fans had shown up to watch the University of Alabama Crimson Tide play the Texas A&M Aggies. It was Week 6 of the 2021 college football season. The date: October 9, 2021.

Texas A&M was unranked. Alabama, on the other hand, was the #1 ranked team in the country. It was a matchup between Alabama Head Coach Nick Saban and Texas A&M Head Coach Jimbo Fisher. The two had been on the same coaching staff in the past as Fisher started coaching under Saban in 2000 as the offensive coordinator and the quarterbacks coach at Louisiana State University. The two of them won a national championship together with LSU in 2003, but the duo's path split when Coach Saban left LSU to coach in the NFL for the Miami Dolphins.

Now their teams would be playing on opposite sides of the ball. Going into this game Texas A&M had a 3-2 record and were on a two-game losing streak. The only Power Five opponent they had beaten was Colorado, a program that had been 1-6 during FBS competition in the season. Alabama had 19 consecutive wins and 100 wins against unranked teams since 2007.

The last time the No. 1 team in the nation lost to an unranked team was 2008. The last time Alabama lost to an unranked team was 2007. On top of that, Coach Saban was 24-0 in beating head coaches who had previously been his assistants.

There was a saying, "Former Nick Saban assistants are 0-for-forever against their old boss." Would this night change everything? Would records be broken or would the Alabama winning streak continue?

The answer would come soon enough. The game kicked off with the Aggies receiving the ball. They drove down the field and were able to strike on that opening drive with a field goal. Aggies on the board: 3-0.

Both teams then traded touchdowns. The Crimson Tide offense started to struggle. Their next two possessions resulted in a fumble and an interception. The Aggies were dominating in the first half and by halftime the score was Texas A&M 24, Alabama 10.

During the second half, both teams kept driving the ball into the end zone and by the end of the third quarter, the Aggies lead was by a touchdown. Texas A&M 31, Alabama 24.

While millions of people watching this game on television, along with many in the stands at Kyle Field, had not expected this type of a score, the game wasn't over yet. There was still fifteen minutes left to play and that was plenty of time for the Tide to pull off a win.

Alabama crept back onto the scoreboard with two more field goals, cutting the lead to just one point. Texas A&M then went three and out. Time to punt back to Bama.

The Tide started moving the ball down the field. With 5:15 left in the game, Alabama quarterback Bryce Young completed a 32-yard pass to Jameson Williams to put them on the Texas A&M 7-yard line. The next play was from Young to Williams for a touchdown. The team went for two and got the two-point conversion. Score: Texas A&M 31, Alabama 38.

As football has shown us time and time again, the game isn't over until the game clock ticks down to 00:00. On the following drive, Texas A&M quarterback Zach Calzada kept things moving, and with 3:00 left in the game, threw a 25-yard pass to Ainias Smith for a touchdown. The game was tied, 38-38.

Alabama couldn't do anything on the next drive and with two minutes left in the game, Texas A&M had a shot to win. The Aggies kept making plays and got the ball down to the Alabama 11-yard line. With 0:02 on the clock the Aggies took a time out. Aggies' kicker Seth Small then kicked a 28-yard field goal. Aggies had done it. They had pulled off a stunning upset and made history. Ainias Smith told me, "The game itself felt like a movie."

Heading into that game, Jimbo Fisher was 0-4 all-time against playing Alabama, with three of the losses as the head coach at Texas A&M and the one other at Florida State in 2017. That night, things changed, and Fisher finally snapped the record and got a win for Saban's coaching tree. Final score: Texas A&M: 41, Alabama 38.

Something that Jimbo Fisher is known for stressing, along with many other coaches and elite athletes, is the importance of *trusting the process*. On the field right before Small kicked the game-winning field goal, Fisher told Small the same thing he always said to Small after a missed kick at practice, "Trust the process. Go back to fundamentals."

On that final play of the game Small was calm, cool, and made a huge kick in a big situation. "It just comes down to us choosing during the week to trust the process," Small said Saturday night after his historic field goal. "That's one thing Coach Fisher told us, 'Don't worry about the scoreboard. Worry about your play, your job on this play, and the scoreboard will be there.'"

Trust the process is something that Coach Saban has said for decades as well. It's an important principle and the players who win on a football field and in life know it all too well.

After that game, Coach Fisher also said, "You have to understand there's a difference of what your results are and what the reality of why those results are there, and then you coach through them. We're doing that, and we're still in the process. Just because we won this game don't fix everything. We've got to learn—prepare and learn to grow from this and understand what we've got to do next week."

The process is a test and it's not about focusing on the outcome. Rather, it's mastering the fundamentals needed for success so that you can consistently show up and achieve the desired results. A life of excellence doesn't occur from winning once, it comes from continually excelling at what you have set out to do. It's about not getting caught up in a single victory and not getting discouraged and quitting when experiencing the losses.

One of my good friends is former professional football quarterback and college football national champion, Chris Leak. In 2003, ESPN's Lemming's Top 100 had Leak listed as the #1 player in the nation. In high school, Chris led his football program to three consecutive NCHSAA Class 4A state championships and lost only one game as a starter. He led the state in passing yardage and touchdowns every year, breaking every state record that existed. He also broke the national record for touchdowns. During Chris' high school career, he set North Carolina state records for passing yards in a career (15,593) and completions in a career (1,013). Additionally, his 185-career touchdown passes set a state record and that also ranked second nationally.

Chris' success continued as he embarked on his college football journey at The University of Florida. During his senior year, Chris led the Gators to their first SEC championship since 2000 and their first national championship game appearance since 1996. In that 2006 BCS Championship Game, Chris led Florida to a 41-14 victory over Ohio State and he was awarded the offensive Most Valuable Player for the game. Chris finished his college career setting the Florida school record with 11,213 career passing yards, a record that he still holds. He also set the school record for total offense yards with 11,350 yards, which has since then only been surpassed by Tim Tebow. Chris is also ranked #3 in Florida Gators history for career touchdowns.

> " The results will come if you give your all to the process." —Chris Leak

Chris and I would talk often about football and one topic that he and I discussed frequently is the importance of trusting the process. Chris has emphasized to me that no matter what you are doing in life you need to keep fighting and trust the process, regardless of the outcome. He said, "I think a lot of times, especially in today's culture, we're so results driven instead of process driven. If you focus on the process, if you fall in love with the process, the results will come. That's one thing I have learned through the process of being a quarterback and understanding the task. The results will come if you give your all to the process."

When you hear people say, "trust the process," I realize that this also is often times easier said than done. An acronym I use when coaching individuals and athletes on trusting the process is to just keep it **REAL**.

R = Remain Connected to Your Why

E = Embrace the Struggle

A = Always Walk in Faith

L = Limit Your Negative Energy

Rule #1: Remain connected to your why.

Achieving greatness requires effort and a whole lot of it. Sleepless nights. Constant grinding. Walking a whole lot of miles sometimes to find out you were just walking in circles. Shedding blood, sweat, and tears. Let's face it—if this were easy everyone would do it.

However, the ones who do make it are the ones who show up ready to play the game and remain focused on their process. In addition to their relentless determination, they remember to remain connected to their purpose.

It is without question that top-tier athletes have a killer work ethic and they put the time in so they can separate themselves from the rest and be the best. While these individuals have achieved incredible accomplishments, they aren't different from the general population when it comes to feelings. They are not immune to or exempt from experiencing unpleasant emotions and, they too, go through the full suite including anger, sadness, disappointment, heartbreak, and frustration.

What keeps them going during these times is their linkage to their why. They never lose sight of their reason for being on the journey and they use that to fuel them through the good, the bad, and the ugly.

Staying connected to your purpose is crucial for your success; your why is going to keep you engaged and on track. It will provide you with inspiration and direction. This connection will be your map for guiding you to achieving your goal. The key for you is to stay connected to your purpose and keeping that alive. Sometimes this purpose can get lost amongst your daily tasks, meetings, and other obligations. Having a physical reminder is a fantastic way to ensure your why is at the forefront of your mind. Then, when life tests you, you can look at your reminder and use that to keep you locked in and sticking with your process.

Rule #2: Embrace the struggle.

When there is no struggle, there is no strength. We need adversities and challenges in our life to grow us and mold us into who we are meant to be. Through life you will face having to do activities that are not sexy, that are tedious, that stretch you, and that quite frankly just suck. But that is all a part of the process and the journey. These cumbersome activities are meant to shape you for your purpose.

The high performers in life understand this and instead of shying away from these experiences, they embrace the suck. They honor the struggle as they deal with the challenges that life throws at them. They show up to each day ready to take on what is necessary so they can continue to move forward.

High performers appreciate that they will need to challenge themselves and welcome any and all struggles with open arms. They don't back down and they play through the suck. They've tightened up their chin strap, secured their cleats, and suited up eager to play the game.

When you are tested and faced with times of adversity, you need to check yourself and your commitment level. Are you still taking ownership over what it is you want to do? If so, that means you embrace the struggle, trust the process, and you keep on swinging each day.

Rule #3: Always walk in faith.

If you haven't figured it out by now, results do not happen overnight. How does the saying go, it takes 10 years to become an overnight success?

The recipe for winning in life includes a of cup of daily productivity mixed in with a heaping tablespoon of consistency and a dash of patience. When blended enough, the breakthroughs and the transformation will come. But how long will that take? That is the million-dollar question. If only we knew. Unfortunately, there is no crystal ball; we know that greatness takes time. A huge part of trusting the process is to always walk by faith and not by sight.

What this means is that you cannot live by the circumstances of what happens in the day-to-day or what you are going through on a daily basis, but rather you need to live by the belief that it will be better one day, and you are going to get through whatever it is you are facing.

When I ventured into the world of full-time entrepreneurship, it was just a few months before the world spiraled into uncertainty and chaos because of the Coronavirus pandemic. I remember being at the NFL Combine during the last week of February 2020. That was when the stock market started to plummet and the Dow Jones Industrial Average (DJIA) dropped by almost 880 points in a single day. That was just the beginning. Businesses started to shut down and March brought on a new wave of volatility. The stock market dropped drastically with multiple days of the DJIA going down by over 1,000 points in a day. It was crazy!

Friends reached out to me asking how I was doing. They knew it had been a substantial decision for me to hang up my corporate cleats, walk away from everything I had been building in my career, and go all-in on growing the Move the Ball brand and the movement. Part of my plan included cashing out on some of my stock holdings to fund my business operations and to pay my living expenses. With the market plunge, a good portion of that money was gone (on paper and I certainly wasn't going to cash out as I believed in the integrity of the market and things would recover). This forced me to get creative with some of my financing.

During conversations with friends, some of them said, "Wow, Jen. This is really bad timing."

You would expect most people to respond to that by agreeing or saying something like "Yeah that sucks." But that wasn't my response.

I said, "No this isn't bad timing. I'm going to get through this and I'm going to have a great story on the other side."

I had wrestled with the decision to leave corporate and now that I made the jump, I sure as heck wasn't going to let this global event stop me from what I set out to do. I stayed true to my faith and knew if I stuck with my process that it would all be ok in the end.

Also, I had just started my *Move the Ball* podcast, which had kicked off the day after Super Bowl LIV and I was paying a company a significant fee to produce my show. The easy thing to do would be to stop the podcast and not incur that monthly expense. I also had a marketing firm that I was playing thousands of dollars each quarter and I could've cut out that expense too. But I chose not to skimp on either.

I knew that both costs were an integral part of building my business and growing my brand. In other words, these expenses were investments and I was unwilling to cut them during a time when it seemed like the world was falling apart. I was not going to let the day-to-day external events stop me or deter me from going after my goal.

According to the Bureau of Labor Statistics, 20% of businesses in the United States fail within the first year. I was determined to not be a part of that statistic. While the pandemic required me to pivot and pivot and pivot some more (isn't that the entrepreneurial way), I was going to show up each day and figure out what I needed to do to continue to progress.

So, how did I do during my first year layered with a pandemic on top of it? I'm proud to share that my first year as a full-time entrepreneur was a six-figure year for me. So, if you ask me, I'll say it wasn't bad timing and I did have a good story to share. Faith over fear. I trusted the process.

Rule #4: Limit the negative energy.

When you push yourself out of your comfort zone and challenge yourself beyond your old limits, you are going to start to feel uncomfortable and things might feel unsettling. While you cannot predict or control certain events or outcomes in your life, what you can do is control how you respond. You don't get rid of the unpleasant events of your past by thinking about or talking about it all the time. You get rid of its effect on you by keeping focused and moving forward.

It is easy to remain fixated on an event or outcome that frustrated you, hurt you, or prevented you from achieving something. What's important to remember though is these things are in the past. It's happened, you cannot change that. If someone wronged you, let it go. If you didn't get the job you wanted, let it go. You can't change what happened. Talking about it to some extent helps as you need to release that negative energy.

Once you've initially processed those emotions, if you continue to remain stuck in the negativity, you are giving that event or that person permission to retain control over you. Those events then control your thoughts, your energy, and what you do going forward. If you spend too much time thinking about "the last play" (i.e., the things that occurred in the past), then you won't be ready for the next one. You cannot let the events of yesterday preclude you from doing what you wanted to do today.

Therefore, you need to limit your negative energy, contain it, and then have the courage to tell yourself, "Today's a new day. I'll try again and I'll continue to move forward." You need to play the next play. Devote all of your focus and energy on your next moves.

Trusting the process and continuing to push forward requires you to have discipline and a relentless mindset. This means never losing sight of the ball and never losing sight of where you are going. It means never taking off the jersey. In "What Color is Your Jersey?" you went through an exercise of defining who you are. Now, you need to remain committed to moving forward and staying locked in. No matter what challenges you face, you have to continue to own your game.

There truly is nothing like getting the hell knocked out of you, either literally or figuratively. Events like that will cause us to evaluate what we stand for and what are values are. They force us to make a choice: *give up or keep going.*

That's when you need to pause, take a break, and decide if you are in this game or not. Are you ready for anything that comes across your route? Life is full of uncertainty and unexpected outcomes. As Tom Hanks' character said in the movie *Forest Gump*, "Life is like a box of chocolates, you never know what you're going to get." You have no control over what barriers will surface as you are moving through life. What you can control is how you react to those situations.

During that initial year of entrepreneurship, whenever I faced an obstacle, I used sound mental toughness coupled with a relentless attitude to press ahead. I was determined to learn from any setback and used that knowledge to make me stronger—mentally, physically, and emotionally.

As another example, during my time in senior management with The Boeing Company, I was in a role where I led a team of complacent employees who had an entitlement mindset. I needed to change things up and do things differently as our customers, and my leadership, were unhappy with the status quo. I was met with strong resistance. Every time I felt we made one step forward, we then took two steps back.

Though it was frustrating, I never lost sight of the goal and trusted my process. I was determined to overcome the barriers that existed. I had never not done the job that was expected of me and I certainly wasn't going to walk away from this one. I was relentless in my pursuit of turning things around. For months, I worked tirelessly. There were nights I wanted to pull my hair out. Slow progress was made, but it was progress, nonetheless. This job tried my patience. It tested me in ways I didn't think possible. But I remained focused and mentally strong. By the time I left that job three years later, I was happy with the results I produced. My customers were pleased and my boss was delighted. I stuck with my process, and it worked.

No matter what you're going through in life, you need to stick with your process and trust the plan. Regardless of how great you think that plan is, things will happen, and you will need to make adjustments. It's important to surround yourself with the right people, as discussed in "Get Inside the Huddle," focus on what you can control, and always live by faith not by sight.

Trust the process, get back to your fundamentals, and put in the work. Don't give up because when you stick with it long enough, the results you are seeking will come. If you want it bad enough, you will find a way to make it happen. Just remember to keep it REAL.

COACH'S CHALKBOARD

1. The process is a test. Stay disciplined.

2. Fall in love with the process, the results will come.

3. Find your purpose and keep pushing.

4. Embrace the struggle.

5. Always walk by faith and not by sight.

6. Control how you respond to situations.

7. Limit your negative energy.

8. Buy into the process, then trust it.

CHAPTER 15:
4TH AND INCHES

*"There is no passion to be found playing small and setting for
a life that is less than you are capable of living."*
—Nelson Mandela

Fourth down moments. They happen on the football field and they happen in business and in life. Fourth downs are decision points. Heck, there was one of them back on January 23, 2011, between the Green Bay Packers and the Chicago Bears that became the inspiration for me to write *Move the Ball*, which is the thing that started the Move the Ball movement and set me on a path I never thought I would be on. Now I'll come back to that NFL game later in the book and if you have already read *Move the Ball* (or have heard my story before), you probably know about that fourth down and what took place.

In the sport of football, when a team gets to a fourth down, they have two choices: *go for it or punt the ball.* Many factors are taken into consideration and the coaches weigh all their options. Time left on the game clock, the scoreboard, the team's field position, and the number of yards needed for a first down are among the many inputs that go into the decision. If things look favorable, such as a 4th and inches or 4th and 1 situation, the team will likely take the risk and go for it. Not always, but in many cases. Conversely, if the risks are too great, or there is significant concern about the team's ability to convert, then they will punt. Now that's the normal decision-making process. There are other times where the team will take the huge risk and go for it even if the odds are against them because it's a must to have a chance of winning the game.

One example of this was during the 2021 NFL season when the Baltimore Ravens played the Detroit Lions at Ford Field. The Ravens were in the direst of dire situations, trailing the Lions by one in the final minutes of the game and they were faced with a 4th down situation. It was 4th and 19 from the Ravens' own 16-yard line with 26 seconds left in the game. The Ravens also had no timeouts left. Had it not been the end of the game, pretty much every football team would punt under these circumstances.

However, here, the Ravens had to go for it. There was no other choice. Ravens quarterback Lamar Jackson let a pass rip down the sideline after some maneuverability where he connected with wide receiver Sammy Watkins for a 38-yard completion. This gave the Ravens a first down and a shot at winning the game. This was a long shot and with three seconds left to play, it looked like the Lions were going to shock the Ravens with an upset.

To win the game, the Ravens were going to have to kick a 66-yard field goal, something that had never been achieved before. This kick was the 22nd time in NFL history that a team had attempted a field goal of 66 yards or more, and prior to this attempt, NFL kickers were 0-21. It didn't look good for the Ravens.

In the final seconds of the game Ravens kicker Justin Tucker ran onto the field. On that last play of the game, Tucker nailed the longest field goal as the ball made it through the uprights by about two centimeters. The kick hit the crossbar and for people watching the game on tv, it wasn't clear if the field goal had made it. The two officials standing in the end zone stared at each other for a few seconds and then declared the kick good, making this dramatic kick the perfect way to end a dramatic game. Final score: Ravens 19, Lions 17.

That 66-yard kick broke the previous NFL record, held by Arizona Cardinals Kicker Matt Prater (which was 64 yards made when Prater was with the Denver Broncos in 2013). Prater and Tucker are the only two kickers in NFL history to land field goals of 64 yards or more.

In this example, there wasn't really a decision point. The Ravens needed to go for the fourth down or they would have lost the game. In life, we usually don't have that kind of forcing function and need to be courageous enough to go for it when its fourth and inches or fourth and long.

One thing that we know about life is that it will continually challenge you. It will put you in situations that test your character and strength. In those scenarios, winners possess the drive, the determination, and the courage to keep going. When the game clock ticks downward, great players press forward. They keep playing the game and take risks to move the ball.

One of my favorite actors is Denzel Washington. Known as one of the best method actors of his generation, Denzel's highly potent and dramatic performances have landed him several awards including multiple Grammy and Academy Awards. His ability to portray intense characters is second to none and being a football girl, I loved his performance in the movie *Remember the Titans*. Aside from being a phenomenal actor, Denzel is an incredible speaker and knows how to engage and inspire others.

During a speech that Denzel once delivered, he said, "I found that nothing in life is worthwhile unless you take risks. Nothing." He continued by emphasizing that tomorrow was never promised, and he shared something that he had heard from world-renowned motivational speaker, Les Brown. That story involved imagining you are on your deathbed and standing around your deathbed are the ghosts representing your unfilled potential—the ghost of the ideas you never acted on and the ghost of the talents you didn't use. They're standing around your bed angry, disappointed, and upset. Those ghosts then tell you they came to you because you could've brought them to life and now all of them must go to the grave together. Do you want your untapped potential to get buried with you? I hope not.

While I recognize this is a morbid example, Denzel continued to ask his audience, how many ghosts are going to be around their death bed. This is something we all need to think about as life is about taking risks. When it comes down to it, we often regret the chances we didn't take. You need to take the shots and see what happens. It isn't always going to work, and you aren't always going to get the win, but as the saying goes, you miss 100% of the shots you don't take.

Did you know that MLB Legend Reggie Jackson, aka "Mr. Outfielder," struck out 2,600 times in his career? This was the most in baseball history. Jackson also hit 563 career home runs and was an American League (AL) All-Star for 14 seasons. During his career, Jackson won two Silver Slugger Awards, the AL Most Valuable Player (MVP) Award in 1973, two World Series MVP Awards, and the Babe Ruth Award in 1977. Something to keep in mind is that you don't hear about the strikeouts, people just remember the home runs and the success. But it all starts with putting yourself out there, taking the swings, and then you just keep on swinging.

Something you might not know about Denzel is his life plan wasn't to be an actor. In fact, he started off in college as a pre-med student. He then switched to pre-law and then to journalism. His GPA was a 1.8 and his school suggested he take some time off. After spending some time working, he found his path to acting. But it wasn't a walk in the park for him and he wasn't on a path to immediate stardom. He put himself out there and didn't get the role time and time again. But he didn't stop taking those risks. He kept showing up, putting himself out there, and then doors started to open. Then more doors and more. The rest is history.

The stories of Denzel and of Reggie Jackson are not just one-off types of stories. There are plenty of other examples I could've chosen to highlight the importance of going for it when faced with fourth down moments and decision points.

Take my story as another example. When I left corporate to be a full-time entrepreneur, I told myself I was always going to play big—I was going to run some huge plays and that I did. Sometimes it was fourth down and I needed to decide what my next move was going to be. Did all those plays work out for me? No. I wish they did. There were more times I went for it where it didn't pan out than did. But that's part of the game and those who know how to play it well realize that.

So, let's talk about those times I went for it, got that "next first down," and kept the ball moving. Those risks I took were worth all the times that they didn't work out. That's what life is about. It's about showing up to every single moment like you belong there, taking the shot, and letting the chips fall where they may. With my business, to have been able to work with very accomplished professional athletes and successful entrepreneurs has been incredible. There are people I never thought in my life I would have the opportunity to work with. It was all because I had the courage to put myself out there and take the risk.

Now it's your turn. The world needs your talents and what you have to offer. We all know that in life if there is no risk, there is no reward. Life will never be a straight path and you get tested the most when it's time to elevate. Everyone has the training and the talent they need to succeed and to win in life, but the question for you is do you have the guts to go for it?

When playing your game, don't break and don't back down from what it is you set out to do. Remember that things can change instantly for you. That's the beauty of life. You are one decision and one unconditional belief away from a new life. You just have to make a decision and take the risk. So, get out there and give it everything you've got. Trust the process and run your plays. No matter what happens, you'll be glad that you did.

COACH'S CHALKBOARD

1. Life is about taking risks. If you never do, you'll never achieve your dreams.

2. When something is important enough, you do it even if the odds are not in your favor.

3. You miss 100% of the shots you don't take.

4. To win big, sometimes you have to take big risks.

5. You'll never be found, if you're not there.

6. Champions keep playing until they get it right.

CHAPTER 16:
WITH OR WITHOUT YOU

*"Life is too short to get bogged down and be discouraged.
You have to keep moving. You have to keep going. Put one
foot in front of the other, smile, and just keep on rolling."*
—Kobe Bryant

"No."

"You're wasting your time."

"What makes you think you know anything about football?"

"If you were my daughter, I'd tell her not to focus on football. Stick with corporate."

These are examples of the types of comments I heard *many* times along my journey when trying to break into the sports industry. Let's keep it real. Are you surprised? Probably not.

I cannot tell you how many people have told me "No" or weren't interested in what the Move the Ball brand represented or the value it could have in sports and working with professional athletes.

Rejection and dismissiveness came over and over and over. Yes, and over some more. But here's the thing to remember: *If you want to chase a path to greatness, you start with defeat, loss, and rejection.*

When you're trying to build or do something great, not everyone is going to be on board with your vision, see your value, or want to be along for the ride. That's ok. Your purpose does not require other's permission, and their affirmation or understanding is not necessary for your progress.

Take any successful entrepreneur's story. Their path is full of rejection, disappointment, heartache, and so much more. But as every successful entrepreneur will tell you, often times you have to hear many "Nos" before you get to the "Yes." That's just a part of life.

It's important to remember that the "Nos" (i.e. those rejections) do not mean you aren't good enough. It means that the person failed to notice what you had to offer. In other words, that individual wasn't meant to be with you on your journey. There's nothing wrong with that. Once you accept that fact, it's easier to let go of those experiences and interactions and continue to move forward. Sometimes too, you'd be surprised when the people who didn't want to be with you on your journey come back years later and want to walk the path with you.

Let me share a quick story on this. I was at an Influencer conference where Jamie Kern Lima shared her journey to build *It Cosmetics* which she eventually sold to *L'Oreal* for $1.2 Billion. Like all of us, her path to success had not happened overnight.

Time after time, Jamie was told "No" by many people. With every "No," she had a choice. She could let that deter her and she could quit, or she could continue with her mission to make *It Cosmetics* into a thriving business and serve the people she created the company for in the first place. Given the sale to *L'Oreal*, you know what path she chose.

Now here's one of the neat parts of this story. One of the head people from QVC (yes, the home shopping channel) who initially told Jaime "No" when she pitched an *It Cosmetics* deal to QVC ended up working for Jaime years later. The lesson is sometimes people will end up coming back in your path down the road, but they aren't meant to be with you today.

When someone doesn't align with your vision or where you want to go, just remember you are going to continue to push for what you are looking to achieve *with or without them.*

Let's be honest for a minute. Rejection isn't fun. It isn't pleasant and it certainly isn't something any of us look forward to. But it is a necessary part of success. Here are some important points to keep in mind when it comes to getting a "No" and facing a rejection.

Point 1: Rejection is merely a redirection.

To highlight this point, I want to tell you about a friend of mine, Darryll Stinson, who is an entrepreneur, pastor, speaker, and suicide survivor. Darryll played defensive end at Central Michigan University and in 2011, attempted to take his life due to an athletic career-ending injury. Through a second chance, he came to believe that his life mattered and began the arduous journey of discovering what his identity and purpose was outside of sports. Now, Darryll is on a mission to help people experience life and live more abundantly.

Darryll joined me during Season 1 of the *Move the Ball* podcast and as part of that conversation we discussed how rejection should be viewed as our friend and not our enemy. He said we should view rejection as projection and protection. When we are rejected from something, what that event is doing is redirecting us to the path we're meant to be on. Those people are not meant to be on the path with us.

We have our why and our purpose. That "why" doesn't really change, but the "what" may change. So as long as you are looking to fulfill your purpose, if you're playing big enough, of course you're going to experience circumstances where there will be rejection. That negative response could be protecting you as there are certain people that are no longer meant to be alongside you moving forward.

The important thing is to not get discouraged by that rejection. Just like Jaime with *It Cosmetics*, every time you get a "No," you have a choice to make *accept that rejection and quit or accept that rejection and recognize it as a redirection and keep going.*

Being rejected sucks. Let's not sugar coat it. When people don't invite you to hang out with them, it feels terrible. Nobody wants to feel left out. When you get on a sales call and don't convert, that's disappointing. If you were to speak at an event and people didn't applaud, that would be awful and probably embarrassing. But when these things happen, that just means we need to do better. We learn from those experiences and we keep pressing on.

Here's another way to view rejection that Darryll shared with me. He said to think of rejection like the coach who's watching football film on you and pointing out your mistakes. There's two ways to view coaching and correction. One way is for someone to take that as "I suck, I don't have what it takes." But coaches don't waste time coaching people who suck and who don't have what it takes. The reason coaches coach is because they see the potential in someone.

Think of rejection as like your million-dollar coach. When rejection happens in your life, it's like you watching film, seeing the mistakes. Picking the wisdom up you see on film and using it to be a better player in life, to be a better spouse, to be a better professional, and to be a better human being. Rejection, while it may feel hurtful at times, it really is helpful and is redirecting you on the path that you are meant to be on.

Point 2: Not everyone is meant to be with you on your journey.

As human beings we want to be liked, we want to be accepted, and we want to feel like we matter. We want others to support our goals and our dreams. For those who are on social media, we want lots of likes and followers. But some people who once liked our content might choose to unfollow us. It happens all the time. While losing followers or not getting the support we were hoping for is a part of life, the important thing to remember is not everyone is meant to be with you on your journey going forward. When you learn to not take that personally and that it's just a part of the way things are, it makes it easier to continue to make progress on whatever it is you have set out to do.

A friend of mine, Brenden Clinton (also known on social media as "Coach 30" and "Mr. Go 30") has done an incredible job building his audience and his brand creating skits that he posts on Instagram, TikTok, YouTube, and Twitter. I've seen him grow his following on these social platforms which includes having a TikTok following of over 785k and over 25M likes on his videos. Brenden was a guest on Season 2 of the *Move the Ball* podcast where we had discussed his progression and success building his brand. During our conversation, he stressed the importance of being consistent in what it is you're doing, even when you're not necessarily getting the likes or the view you want on social media.

Whether it's a lack of social media views and likes on content you're creating, or a lack of support outside of the digital space, Brenden hits the nail on its head with emphasizing consistency which has been a theme throughout this book. You need to be consistent in whatever it is you're looking to achieve, whether you have the following or support you want or not. You are going to reach your goals with or without them as long as you keep being consistent and putting the work in.

Now, I understand how certain people not wanting to support you can be upsetting. Striving for greatness isn't always easy and it can be hard when we had relationships where we expected people to stick with us and have our backs, so to speak. As I've gotten older, I've come to realize that there's a time and place for certain people and relationships in our life, and unfortunately for some of those connections, they weren't meant to be forever.

Let me share one such interaction that disturbed me. As an entrepreneur and business owner, I spend a lot of time on social media platforms, and I enjoy networking with other professionals. One platform I use quite a bit is LinkedIn. A few years back I connected with an executive in a Fortune 500 company and enjoyed having him as part of my professional network. This individual ended up signing up for my mailing list and for a couple of years had been receiving my emails.

One day, I had a glitch with my contact management system and an old e-mail went out to my audience that wasn't supposed to be sent out. Whoops! When I found out, I freaked out and I was embarrassed.

"What do I do now?" I thought to myself.

I decided to send another email out letting people know that the original message had been a mistake. In that second email, I also wanted to turn it into a teaching/motivational moment, so I mentioned how I panicked after I found out the initial message was sent, that I was human, and I make mistakes just like anyone else. The messaged continued with how when things like this happen, we can't let it ruin our day, we need to just keep moving forward.

There were some people who responded to my message telling me not to worry about it, things happen, and it was no big deal. But this one individual, we'll call him Jake, wasn't one of those people. Jake sent me a message, but it wasn't a pleasant one.

Jake told me that he thought my e-mail was the fakest of emails and he said "for that, instead of being rude, I will just disconnect our connect here and unfollow you. I am truly disappointed."

There was more in his message and I was completely taken aback by this and quite upset. People who know me know that I pride myself on being very genuine and authentic. His note rattled me so much that I was in tears.

I reached out to a few other friends on my mailing list to ask them if they thought my message came across as fake or ingenuine. They didn't see it that way at all and because they could tell I was upset, they tried to comfort me.

One of my good friends, Melahni Ake (founder of the *Everyday Leaders* movement) said something to me that happened to make things better. She said, "not everyone is meant to be on the journey with you." When I heard this, it immediately reminded me that this is something I also say to people often. In that moment, I realized it was okay that Jake no longer wanted to follow me or be connected to me. He had been in my life for a certain period, but now that time had expired, and he was no longer meant to continue with me. As my friend, retired NFL player and #1 overall NFL Draft Pick, Irving Fryar, once said to me, "Too often, we try to make people permanent in our lives when they are only meant to be temporary."

When you accept that people in your life are there for a purpose, and that purpose may come to an end, it makes it simpler to emotionally let it go, stay focused, and continue to move forward. After Melahni and I had spoken, it made it easier to forget about Jake and just focus on the next plays I needed to worry about. Now I will share that I did reply to Jake's message, but he never responded. So, I did try to repair the relationship or clear up any misunderstanding, but he made his decision that he wanted to sever ties and that's that.

Point 3: You can't listen to the noise and the negativity of others.

In my consulting and speaking work, I get to interact often with college and professional athletes. With social media being as prevalent as it is now, these young men and women are always in the public eye. With the spotlight on them 24/7 and people having tons of courage behind a keyboard, the opinions posted online, or tweets tweeted, about these athletes can be brutally cruel.

But do you think these players pay attention to all of this negativity? Of course not, they can't. Let me share another story about my friend, Mickey Joseph, who served as the Interim Head Football Coach at Nebraska during the 2022 college football season, making him the first African-American head coach of any sport in Nebraska school history. Mickey had joined me on Season 2 of my podcast when he was on the Louisiana State University football coaching staff. Mickey had been the Wide Receivers Coach and an Assistant Head Coach when LSU won the CFP National Championship during the 2019 college football season. On the show, Mickey discussed how he stresses to his players that they can't listen to everything the fans and people on social media are saying. This is because there will even be times when the fans who are clapping one game will be right out there another day saying a player needs to sit on the bench if they don't play good in a game.

He emphasized that he tells his kids to be mindful of what social media battles they engage in and that they need to just block out all of that noise that's online so they can stay focused on performing every single day, both on and off the field. The same is true for everyone, whether they are a college or professional athlete, public figure, influencer, or everyday Joe or Jane.

On the road to success, you will run into naysayers and haters, people who might be social media trolls or others who want to impede your progress. In a nutshell, you need to push them to your sideline. Don't even give them the time of day. I say this because if you take the time to defend yourself, or to go on the offensive, you just play into their hands. That's exactly why they express these opinions, they want to elicit a response. They want that attention. That attention only nourishes those naysayers, so don't feed into that. Additionally, what you're doing is you're not only giving them extra motivation to continue to do that toward you, you're expending unnecessary energy and taking time away from working on those things that you need to be homing in on.

Remember, time is precious. Every minute you spend dealing with these naysayers, those minutes are now gone. You can never get them back. There's no rewind, replay, they're gone. So instead of spending them on these people that don't matter, focus your time and your effort and your energy on those tasks and activities that really are going to help you move forward.

I'll just share when you look at some of history's most notable and influential figures, such as Martin Luther King, Jr., Mahatma Gandhi, and Nelson Mandela, these three individuals persevered despite intense criticism and opposition. They didn't allow others' negativity to deter them from their missions. You need to do the same thing.

One more point to keep in mind is the reason these people hate on others is because they are unhappy with themselves. They deal with this by attacking others. So, if you choose not to acknowledge them, that's good, because you're not allowing them to project their own unhappiness onto you. And this allows you to just focus on yourself.

> *If you accept the negative expectations of others, you will never change the outcome."*
> *—Michael Jordan*

Along the lines of naysayers and negativity, aside from these people, the world just has negativity around it. You see the news, there's all kinds of negative things happening here and there, those things can drag you down. So, with the naysayers, the haters, and just the negativity in the world, you just need to vibrate higher.

This is a theme I use a lot because you need to vibrate above the noise and then surround yourself with people who are going to uplift you and really help you stay motivated and make those key plays. This will also help you to ignore the opinions of those who don't matter and remain locked in on your objectives. The affirmations of others are not necessary for your progress. You don't need anyone else's permission and don't let someone else stop you from chasing a dream. You're going to do it without them.

Once you believe in yourself anything is possible. I'm living proof of that and there are so many other stories that I could point to that drive that point home too. No matter how hard it gets, never give up. Surround yourself with the people that want to be with you on the journey and let the reason why you started be the reason that you don't quit. The right doors will open and the right people will come to you when you stay true to your purpose and who you were meant to be. Keep showing up when others would throw in the towel and prove all the doubters wrong. Your spark needs to stay ignited, keep shining your light bright, and you will move the ball.

COACH'S CHALKBOARD

1. Chase your dreams, not approval.

2. Do not feel the need to entertain those who doubt you.

3. Ignore the opinions of those who are irrelevant.

4. When someone doesn't believe in you, realize that their understanding or affirmation is not necessary for your progress.

5. Forget the naysayers. Tune out the noise.

CHAPTER 17:
MANAGE THE GAME CLOCK

"Learn to differentiate between what is truly important and
what can be dealt with at another time"
—Mia Hamm

8 6,400. 1,440. 525,600. The first and second numbers represent the number of seconds and minutes in each day, respectively. The third equals the number of minutes in a 365-day calendar year. Yes, you get a few more minutes during a leap year, 1,440 more!

These numbers tie to your daily and yearly game clock. If you want to accomplish the things in life that really matter, then you need to show up each day the right way and play your game on offense. Don't let the game play you and be in a defensive and reactive mode. This isn't the first time I've said this.

Most people go through life on autopilot without giving any thought as to what happens each day. They are the players who are merely running on survival mode—they just take each day as life throws things at them. In other words, they are not purposeful and deliberate about how they spend their energy, or their time, and they lack a roadmap or a plan as to how they should prioritize their day.

If you were to ask these individuals about the three numbers from above, they would be clueless. They aren't focused on their game clock and they certainly are not managing their time effectively.

Football teams know all about the importance of clock management.

It can play a critical factor in determining the winner of the game. Proper clock management requires teams to play the game at a certain speed or to use a specific strategy to use the clock to the team's advantage.

If a team is winning, their objective is to run out the clock or run as much time off the clock as possible. They might get in and out of the huddle slowly, will often run the ball instead of passing it, the players will try to stay in bounds, and the team will use the entire play clock before the ball gets snapped. If a team is losing and the game clock is running low, a team can employ a hurry up offense, which is a faster-paced offensive than they normally would use, and they will try to run out of bounds as often as possible to stop the clock. These are all effective strategies for a team to try and end up victorious when the game clock hits 00:00.

If you are an avid sports fan, I'm sure you can think of a time when your sports team might have been trailing and had to manage the game cock so they could still put points on the board and have a shot at winning the game.

One example that comes to mind is Super Bowl LI between the Atlanta Falcons and the New England Patriots. It was February 5, 2017, and these two teams were playing at NRG Stadium on professional football's largest stage. Fox's broadcast of the game averaged 111.3 million viewers. What a show that game turned out to be.

The first quarter was a scoreless defensive match resulting in each team punting the ball twice. Things heated up in the second quarter where Atlanta scored three touchdowns to take a 21-3 halftime lead, which they then increased to 28-3 midway through the third quarter. Based on how strongly they were playing, the Falcons were surely going to be the Super Bowl LI champion.

Wait a minute though. We know nothing is guaranteed in football. The Patriots then ended up scoring 25 unanswered points to tie the game in the final seconds of regulation. In overtime, New England received the kickoff after winning the coin toss and scored a touchdown to win the game. The Patriots had overcome the largest deficit in Super Bowl history and won the only Super Bowl in an overtime period. There were a lot of factors that contributed to Tom Brady and the Patriots being victorious that night, but proper game clock management also played a significant part.

While you aren't suited up on a football field, it is still important that you practice proper game clock management, that is, the time you have to play your game each day. These four strategies are ones you will want to incorporate into your playbook to ensure you utilize your time effectively and in a productive manner.

COACH'S PLAYBOOK

1. Plan it Out (Get Organized)

2. Block Time (Undivided Attention to Tasks)

3. Optimize Your Environment (Limit Distractions)

4. Use the Power of No (Be Selective)

Strategy #1: Plan out your schedule each day.

To be in the one percent means that you are a super high performer. To operate at this level, you need to manage that game clock and spend your time ultra-effectively. One strategy to achieve this is to plan out your schedule each day. The first thing is you should map out your plan for each week. Previously, I shared that I do this on Sunday nights. I figure out what my priorities are for the week and then I schedule the tasks into the days accordingly.

The next part of this is managing your day starting at the beginning of the day. When you wake up in the morning, you should not do what most people do. What is it that majority of individuals do after they get out of bed and brush their teeth?

They open their laptop or they check their phone. Did you know it is proven by science that if you check your inbox or any social media in the first thirty or sixty minutes each day, your productivity goes down by thirty percent? That is because when you do this, you are checking into the world's needs, its fire alarms, its challenges, and its false emergencies. Remember, when you "check in" to the inbox and social media or your phone, you are "checking into" that world and giving others permission to steal your time and your energy.

When you do this, you are going into reactive mode. You are checking out of strategic living. You are checking out of proactivity and entering the world of reaction. Then what happens is you check into other people's agenda and you're responding to their needs and desires. Day after day, week after week, month after month, your life becomes a life of reaction. People who live this way never achieve a life that is legendary.

Instead of checking into the world, the first thing you need to do is to revisit your daily plan as this will help set the tone and position you for the rest of the day. This is part of what I do in my morning routine as part of my Power Hour that I mentioned in another chapter. You want to use your time to focus on your strategy and your playbook. When you have done this, you will have taken ownership over your game, and you'll be on your way to managing your game clock effectively.

Ask yourself: *What do I really need to get done today?*

This is the big picture stuff, don't get into the tiny little weeds. No kidding, what must happen today? You should have a list of 3-5 things that must happen today so you can move forward. Write them down and prioritize them as that is your focus for the day. Everything else comes second and only as you have time.

The next step is identifying who on your team you can leverage to make sure you get what you need to complete those tasks. When you look at your inbox, you then filter by who has sent you stuff, and you search for the emails from the people you need input from to complete the items on your list for the day. If you don't have an email from them on what you need, then don't read all the other emails. Reach out to those people right away so you can get them working on what you need to get your stuff done today.

I'm at a point in my life where I don't say, "Oh I forgot to email that person." Because the first thing I do in the day is email all the people I need to hear from on something. It's part of my morning routine. Now that you have strategically mapped out your game plan for the day and reached out to your teammates, you need to focus on playing your position and knock out the critical activities you've identified for that particular day. Then you can reply to other emails and respond to people as you have bandwidth. But you prioritize your critical tasks first. This will keep you on track and you will be using your time the right way and not operating in a reactive mode.

Strategy #2: Schedule blocks of time for critical activities each day.

An effective strategy to being productive is to schedule 45 minutes of "block time" in your day that is dedicated for you to do work, advance ideas, think, or do whatever you need to do to move the ball forward. You don't check your phone, alerts, alarms, nothing. Inbox is closed. All you are doing is focusing on a specific task or set of tasks. That's it.

You need to pick 45-minute blocks of time uninterrupted. While you don't need to do this for every 45-minute increment throughout the day, it is recommended to have at least three. This is for your creative contribution to do work you need to get done. All you are doing is focusing on the specific tasks you scheduled for that block until they are completed.

Think of it like a sprint (yes, it's longer than a sprint), but all you are doing is focusing on the things you need to get done without distraction or interruption. The more creative and effective you get in your life, the more these blocks should happen.

For example, great writers take significant blocks of time, uninterrupted, to write. They spend 45 minutes here, 45 minutes there, and again and again throughout each day. You might be wondering why it is a 45-minute period and not a full hour.

After this 45-min slot, you will want to stop what you are doing and take a break. Call a quick timeout, stand up, get some water, and stretch. Do something that opens up your body, maybe even take a quick walk. It's scientifically proven that if you take these breaks then you will have less stress and you will be more productive. You need to take these breaks.

When you do this, you'll become more effective, more creative, and yes you will get more done. It's also been scientifically proven that the mind doesn't work well over 90-minute periods of time. So, these breathers are necessary for prolonged productivity and effectivity.

You can even schedule block time to just respond to emails. But during this time, you are crushing the emails. You aren't tweeting or posting on Instagram or Facebook. This is dedicated email time. Whatever that chunk of time is scheduled for, that's what you work on. Now if you get done early, sure you can take a break and use the rest of the time to respond to emails or to check into the social media world. But that is only after you have effectively completed what you scheduled yourself to do. Those other things are your reward *only* after you have performed on what needed to get done.

Strategy #3: Optimize your environment to be most productive.

Your environment can help or hinder your productivity. Therefore, it's your job to optimize your environment and make sure you are in a setting where you can be most productive. It's important to be aware of technology especially, such as your email or messenger that keeps pinging you because someone has messaged you. One suggestion I tell my coaching clients is to turn off notifications, put your phone far away from you, and don't look at emails when you are focused on your critical tasks or priority projects. Checking social media, conducting internet "research" that leads you far off track from what you are doing, responding to emails, and answering phone calls can all lead to distraction and procrastination.

During your scheduled block time, close your email and IM, turn off your phone (or at least set it on "Do Not Disturb" and put it out of sight), and don't let yourself get on the web or check your phone until you have completed the task, or hold off from any necessary internet searches until the end.

When I'm in my scheduled block times, I tend to be deliberate about not having any mobile devices around me. Occasionally, I will get a little lax and the phone will be next to me on the table. When there's a chime on my phone, I may look over at it, but one thing I am very disciplined about is I will not respond to the notification. I'll see it come in and I'll tell myself that I'm busy doing something important and that I'll get to it later.

It could be a Facebook message or LinkedIn message or someone commenting on one of my posts. Regardless of the platform, what I'm not going to do is immediately engage. I'm not going to check into someone else's world simply because I received a notification. I'll be very strategic as to when I will respond. I'll get to it when I have time carved out for responding or when I'm *not* in the middle of something that is the priority. I stay locked in on what it is I'm doing.

This is a very important practice because every time you react to something means you have now taken time away from whatever it is you are supposed to be focused on. The minutes tick away and before you know it, you've wasted ten or fifteen minutes, maybe more. Then you're sitting there wondering where the time went and you're now flustered because you still haven't completed the task you set out to do. The easiest thing to do is to not have the phone around you or your e-mail open when you are locked in on activities.

Optimize your environment to minimize distractions and to tune-out the noise. Shut off the technology to reduce distractions and keep you focused. In today's world of notifications, being able to stay focused is a competitive advantage. Make your environment work for you.

Strategy #4: Say "NO" often.

How many times have you heard yourself saying "Yes" to the wrong things—overwhelming requests, bad relationships, time-consuming obligations? How often have you wished you could summon the power to turn them down?

Well, you can. You hold that power and when you exercise it, your life will change. Saying "No" to the things that don't align with your assignment and your goals is how you can reclaim your time and energy.

A lack of focus leads to a lack of progress. So, you need to stop getting distracted by things that have nothing to do with your goals for each day, each week, each month, etc. Your objective is to remain focused on the things that are important for you today and limit what takes your energy away from those things.

Throughout this book I have discussed this notion of playing the long game. That means setting yourself up for excellence, not exhaustion. For excellence, not mediocrity. As previously mentioned, playing this long game means not just taking life as it shows up; it means being that quarterback and driving the ball in the direction you want to go. Positioning yourself for that life of excellence requires you to say "No" to the things that aren't helping you get closer to the goal line. You must be thinking and playing strategically here.

Someone recently asked me, "How do you seem to have 27 hours in the day when the rest of us only have 24?"

Obviously, I don't have more time than everyone else. Although that would be nice, wouldn't it? Unfortunately, I don't have a genie or a magic lamp. Dang it. While I don't have extra time in the day, what I do have is more of my 24 hours available to work on the *right* things because I exercise the power of "No" more often than I say "Yes" to people and to possible opportunities. I've very purposeful with who and what I am willing to give my time to.

While this holds true now, that wasn't always the case. When I was in my twenties, I always signed up for activities and took on new projects because I enjoyed being busy and knew I could handle anything. Yes, I thought I was invincible. What this resulted in was me being tired all the time, I was overcommitted, and I was often stressed out.

Now that I am older, wiser, and have been saying "No" to things, I am able to manage my game clock much more effectively and get the right tasks done each day. I don't feel like I am trying to cram everything in, and consequently I have considerably reduced my feelings of being overwhelmed and I have controlled that stress factor too.

This holds true even more so as an entrepreneur. When I left my corporate life behind, that was when I felt the pressure of the game clock even more. As an entrepreneur, either you are spending time on activities that are making you money or you aren't. Everything falls on you. There is no "fat" like in a big company where if things take longer, you still get paid. Nope. Not at all. If you aren't focused on the right things as an entrepreneur, you don't get the check. It's just that simple. You feel that pain too.

> *Your daily income is 86,400 seconds. Make sure you spend it wisely.*

You realize the value of every second and of every minute of each day. You pay attention to those minutes and are much more intentional with how you spend that time. You make sure you spend it wisely. As an entrepreneur, I now say "No" to much more than what I say "Yes" to. If an opportunity doesn't align with my brand or coincide with the strategies that I am currently focused on for my business, then it isn't something I will even entertain now. Perhaps there could be a time in the future where an opportunity makes sense to explore, but I'll revisit it when the timing could be right.

This concept isn't a hard one to grasp, but the challenge is putting it into practice. So how do you do make it work for you? First, you need to be mindful of what things are demanding your time. Second, you need to qualify if that activity or person deserves your time and attention today or if it's something that needs to be addressed later. Maybe it's important, but it's not a priority for today. Then you say "No" for today and work on it tomorrow, the next day, or when it really needs to be completed.

One other way to exercise the power of "No" is to not respond to social media messages or texts. I'm constantly getting messaged, but as mentioned earlier, I'm deliberate as to when I respond. If I'm busy and in the zone, I'm not going to stop what I'm doing just to respond. I control when I'm willing to let people come into my space and consume my time and energy. Every time you stop to respond, it ends up being a distraction, which makes you less productive.

One other thing to remember is that you always have the right to say "No" to things, and you should. Say "No" to anything that is hurting you or distracting you. Say "No" to standards that no longer serve you. Say "No" to people who drain you of your creativity and your expression. Say "No" to things that don't align with your core and your vision. Try out this *Power of "No"* for a week and I promise you'll see changes in your life and how much additional time you have to get things done each day.

There you have it. Four strategies in your playbook that will help you to manage your game clock more effectively and set you up for success each day, week, month, and year. When you've planned out your schedule in advance, you're going to be able to show up to each day with more confidence and ready to hit the ground running. Knowing what you need to focus on for the day will help eliminate anxiety and procrastination. Optimizing your environment and getting those block times scheduled will also improve your productivity.

When you see your progress, the momentum will only continue and you'll also find it easier to say "No" to the people and activities that don't align with your priorities. Once you implement these four plays, you'll be eliminating distractions, become more focused, and you'll have additional time each day to play your game and to get you across your goal line. You'll be efficiently managing your game clock and setting yourself up to win.

COACH'S CHALKBOARD

1. Time is not refundable. Spend it wisely.

2. Always ask yourself if what you're doing today is getting you closer to where you need to be.

3. Play your position, plan out your days, and make sure they are productive.

4. Schedule uninterrupted block time into your daily routine.

5. Optimize your environment for success.

6. The Power of No is forceful if you use it purposefully.

7. Know when to say "No."

8. Do not confuse being busy with being productive.

CHAPTER 18:
WIN EVERY DAY

"I think that at the start of a game, you're always playing to win, and then maybe if you're ahead late in the game, you start playing not to lose. The true competitors, though, are the ones who always play to win."
—Tom Brady

Life is complicated. Let's face it. Things aren't always simple, easygoing, comfortable, or straightforward. There will be many moments where we experience joy, love, and laughter, but there will also be those times where we shed tears, feel anger, and go through heartache. We all have different situations that we deal with in life, but the real question you need to consider is this: *Are your circumstances part of a story you tell yourself when things don't work out, or are you intentional with your decisions and are you living a life without excuses?*

In other words, when you take a hard look at your life are you a product of your circumstances, or are you a product of your decisions?

Do you try to justify adversity and your situation as a reason why you aren't getting closer to your goals? Or are you living with intention and managing your daily game clock to its maximum?

I can't tell you how many times people have reached out to me who are still blaming external circumstances for their current situation. They lack ownership and would rather sit idle, continuing to play the victim instead of taking action to make a positive change. Then they share how they are upset and frustrated because they aren't getting the results they want in their life. But the reality is, it's because they didn't put in the work to achieve those desired outcomes.

Everyone has struggles and challenges, but those who become successful in life are the ones who refuse to remain stuck, have a high level of non-acceptance, and are willing to "run plays" to rewrite the script of their lives. They are action takers, plain and simple.

One common trap people fall into is thinking their past is a limitation on their future potential and what that next chapter could look like. Imagine how much better your life would be if, instead of obsessing over the past or worrying about the future, you just suited up and fully showed up ready to win the day—doing this not just today, but every day. Focusing on succeeding in the present is the best formula for winning and living the life that you've been wanting. The things you have done until now have led you to where you are today. But everything you decide to do moving forward will determine where you end up tomorrow.

You recently heard the saying that *tomorrow is promised to no one*. (Hint: It was in Chapter 2). Tomorrow is never guaranteed, for any of us. Therefore, it is important that we manage the clock and the minutes we've been given today so we can claim some wins in the here and now.

Every day is a gift and it's important that we wake up each morning fully aware of that and ready to win those first few hours of the day. Throughout this book, I have stressed the importance of being deliberate about how you show up each day. That means making choices around your mindset, your energy, and consciously engaging in behaviors that lead to habits that lead to your desired outcomes.

When you wake up in the morning, do you hit the snooze button five times? Or do you wake up ready to take on a new day? Do you have a morning routine or are you a dragging like a zombie just lucky enough to even get a shower in without being late?

Beginning with a purpose sets the tone for the day. It's been previously discussed that you should have a morning routine that works for you. While ditching those "old clothes" for new ones might not be easy at first, when done consistently over time, you'll begin to see the positive impact it will have on your productivity, mood, and energy.

Feeding your mind in the morning is also a great way to start off the day. Carve out some time in the morning to listen to your favorite podcasts or read a chapter in a book that enlightens and inspires you, or that provides you with growth. Just as our bodies need food, our minds need proper nourishment. Make sure you're learning something new every day and consuming content that makes you grow holistically. The more positive content and enriching messages you consume, the better and more fruitful your days will be.

It's important to make the choices each morning so you can accomplish even the tiniest of tasks before noon so you can claim a victory. That small, initial win will get you fired up to want to continue to get more wins throughout the day. You'll be energized and your momentum will build and carry you throughout the day.

Remember it's the small, daily improvements and victories that are key to achieving long-term staggering results. It's the consistent action you take that will improve your situation and help you achieve success. Sometimes we focus on making monumental moves, and when those moves don't occur or we don't get the outcome we want, then we get discouraged.

Instead of feeling fully deflated, what we need to do is get fixated on what action we can take each day to make incremental progress. Five small wins each day equals 1,825 wins in a year. Every little win adds up, so don't discount those little successes. One time during a speaking engagement, I mentioned this and someone raised their hand and said, "It's all about the big wins," emphasizing how we should focus on those. Don't get me wrong, big wins are important too.

Keep in mind that sometimes we can't do big wins. We can, though, take little steps each day to improve and knock out smaller tasks to advance. The forward progress is what's important. Whether you move two feet or ten yards in one day, what matters is that you're getting closer to the goal line. Big steps or small steps each day, you decide. Your speed doesn't matter, forward is forward. Don't let people discourage you because you might be moving at a slower pace.

5 small wins each day leads to 1,825 wins each year.

You can't compare your progress to someone else's, as everyone has different situations and circumstances in their life. Focus on the smaller wins, starting in the morning and keep those wins coming throughout the day. Don't forget to honor those small wins too.

Celebrating your wins is all about honoring the small steps, the initial steps towards achieving your goals. This is important, because sometimes you don't recognize yourself and your hard work for those little things.

There are many days where you do a kick-ass job, knock off tasks from your to-do list, you do two or three things that stretch or push you, and maybe you also add some creativity and flair to the world. You know you crushed the day and so you have a glass of wine and celebrate with your favorite meal. Maybe you take a walk or share with your friends, whatever it is that you do to share your excitement of what you've accomplished. You feel pretty good about yourself and you take some time to enjoy yourself.

Then there's other days where you still have been productive, crossed off some key tasks from your whiteboard, but at the end of the day, you just get ready for bed without acknowledging or recognizing all your hard work.

It's about acknowledging the small, initial steps, and the little things towards achieving our goals. So many people lack confidence because they're waiting for a big win before they ever allow that win to be integrated into their identity. When was the last time you really gave yourself credit? When was the last time you really celebrated just a small little thing? What did you do and how did you celebrate it? Take a few minutes and think about this.

If you feel like this is an area that has been lacking and there can be some improvement, here are a few tips to help you to continue to appreciate and honor the mini wins each day so you can really see how you are winning.

The first one is to create a review schedule. One thing that competitive athletes do is they set aside time to review game film to evaluate their performance. They look at what went right and what mistakes or missteps transpired. They also use it for preparing for future games against opponents and more. What's important in my analogy is athletes carve out time for review. You also need to schedule a review timeslot in your day. Take five to ten minutes, or more if you like, to reflect and count the wins you've racked up for the day. Consistency is a good thing, so if you can schedule the same time block each day, that's preferred. But make sure you are factoring in time to recognize yourself for all your hard work on a consistent basis. You should also schedule time during the week to do a week-in-review and again reflect on all the wins you've accumulated.

It's important to actually block this time off in your schedule. Put it in your phone, your outlook calendar, or your planner. You need to schedule it, because if there's not a set time where you are sitting down and reflecting on the wins, then you're not likely to celebrate those small wins in a way that you really should. Some questions you should ask yourself during your weekly review are:

- *What did I achieve this week?*

- *What went well this week?*

- *What things could've happened that I didn't even anticipate?*

- *How can I feel good about something that happened this week?*

- *What brought me joy or fulfillment, and a sense of accomplishment this week?*

I want to emphasize the importance of scheduling a weekly review, to again, take credit for all the wins you've racked up. This is important no matter what's going on in your life. Especially if you are in a period of transition, chaos, or uncertainty, this is even more critical to help keep your momentum going.

I want you to think about when your review time is going to be. Get out a piece of paper or a sticky note and write it down. Then I want you to stare at that paper. I want you to commit to blocking that time off in your schedule every week. Celebrating your wins each week will keep you focused. You'll want to show up and win each day.

I've shared that I do my weekly planning on Sunday nights. This is when I do my weekly review as well. On Sundays, I assess the previous week and ask myself about ten questions. Not only am I reflecting on my progress, but I'm also thinking about what things I should be doing the following week to continue to make me better and keep on winning. I'll also think about how I can celebrate if I achieve certain milestones for the upcoming week.

When you put this review schedule into practice on a weekly basis, what you'll notice is you'll have more energy, feel more joy, gain more confidence, and increase your momentum to keep pushing and tackling those activities and projects you need to complete each day and each week. Do this and do it consistently!

The second suggestion centers around embracing the win. This means actually feeling your wins each day. This is not a check-the-box exercise, but means you relive the small wins, feel them, and integrate them into your life. This helps with generating extra confidence. So, when you're doing your review schedule, think about your wins for the day and then just allow that heartfelt, deep connection to the satisfaction and fulfillment that comes with recognizing yourself.

Step into the moment and really feel your daily accomplishments. You can even make it fun like a game by assigning points to different kinds of tasks and things you get done each week. Then, have different weekly reward levels to treat yourself and to celebrate your progress. Just a suggestion.

Personal development does not have to feel like drudgery. Growth doesn't have to be super painful. Make it exciting. Implement a creative point system and have fun with this. It's important to take joy in the smallest things. Having that joy spurs on curiosity to what other things you can do. As already mentioned, it brings added confidence, too. Allow yourself to really connect to the hard work you have been engaged in each day.

The last tip is to share your wins with friends. This is something super simple, but it's very important. Celebrating the small successes with your friends helps you feel more satisfaction and honors your efforts. It allows you to share with people who love you and want to see you succeed in life. There are so many people who don't take time to share their accomplishments with people in their inner circle because they don't think these little things matter. But they do. Learn how to share what you're doing in life with real enthusiasm.

There's a difference between bragging and just taking a quick minute to celebrate successes in life with other people. We need to share these positive wins, especially when there is so much negativity in the world. So, make sure you're sharing with your friends. Take pride and joy in what you've accomplished. Remember to feel it, really embrace it, and then be sure to share it. You can even post on social media and in your Instagram or Facebook (yes Meta) stories, as an example.

A big part of winning each day is not only completing the things you planned to do, but it's also honoring and acknowledging yourself for putting in the work that day. Claim that credit. When celebrating both small and big wins become part of your practice, you're going to notice that you'll be more energized each day, and you'll give the next day an extra dose of effort because you want to win then too.

Each day, pause, reflect, and give thanks as this is integral to your motivation and to your sense of achievement. Start reconnecting with your achievements and your accomplishments. Start re-engaging with the small steps and you'll find you'll be on your way to more success and to achieving bigger things in life. Outrageous goals coupled with baby steps equals the recipe for success. Don't discount the little things you're doing to move forward.

Remember, each morning starts a new page in your story. It's a page you won't get to re-write. Today only happens once, make it amazing.

COACH'S CHALKBOARD

1. Either you're kicking ass each day or each day is kicking you.

2. You are in control of your life and what you do today.

3. If you don't try to create the future you want, you end up enduring the future you get.

4. Play to win—every day.

5. Suit up, show up, and win the mornings.

6. Your speed doesn't matter. Slow progress is still progress.

7. Small wins, big wins. They all matter.

8. Celebrate your wins each day.

CHAPTER 19:
CONTROL THE "S" FACTOR

"The simplest change in perspective can change a life."
—Oprah Winfrey

Chasing greatness can be demanding. It's constantly uncomfortable, too, because you're hustling and grinding all day, regularly testing new boundaries, and pushing yourself beyond the limits you once put on yourself. Oh, and let's not forget when you're pursuing those big, hairy, audacious goals (yes, the BHAGs), there's normally a whole lot of uncertainty around whatever it is you are trying to do.

I get it. Things can get super taxing. I've been there before, many times. So, while you're out there challenging yourself to keep the ball moving each day, each week, each month, one thing you need to be intent on doing is *Controlling the "S" Factor*. That's right: the *Stress*.

What exactly is stress? It's the natural, physical, and mental reaction you have to life experiences. It is anything from everyday responsibilities like work assignments and family obligations to serious life events such as a new health diagnosis, getting divorced, or the death of a loved one. Stress is something we all encounter from time to time. For some people it occurs more frequently than others. Since this is something we all go through on some level, the focus of this chapter is giving you some tools to control and limit the stress you feel when dealing with the challenges life tosses at you.

Keep in mind for immediate, short-term situations, stress *can* be beneficial to your health. It can help you cope with potentially serious circumstances. Your body responds to stress by releasing hormones that increase your heart and breathing rates and readies your muscles to respond, if needed. But if your stress response doesn't stop firing, and these stress levels stay elevated far longer than is necessary for survival, then it can take a significant toll on your health and can affect your overall well-being. This is not what we want.

There are so many negative effects and issues that prolonged levels of stress can cause and I want to highlight a couple of examples here just so you can understand the severity of how the "S" factor can be detrimental to your health.

When your body is dealing with the stress response, you breathe faster in an effort to quickly distribute oxygen-rich blood to your body. If you already have a breathing problem like asthma or emphysema, it can make it even harder to breathe.

Under stressful situations, your heart also pumps faster. Stress hormones cause your blood vessels to constrict and divert more oxygen to your muscles, so you'll have more strength to act. But this also raises your blood pressure. As a result, frequent or chronic stress will make your heart work too hard for too long. When your blood pressure rises, so do your risks for having a stroke or a heart attack.

These are just a couple of examples and merely scratches the surface of how your body can respond when subjected to sustained stress. While some stress is going to happen in life, that's inevitable, there are things you can do to limit how much of it you experience. You're probably familiar that meditation and physical exercise can help reduce stress, so that isn't going to be covered here, but put these other three principles into practice and you'll find it easier to deal with the day-to-day challenges and whatever life events may surface in your future.

Principle #1: Decide not to be stressed.

Throughout this book, I have constantly mentioned that you get to make choices every single day. One of those choices can be the decision to not be stressed. At some point in our lives, we need to draw a line in the sand and there needs to be an intentional decision where we say we are not going to be too stressed out. You need to "play on offense" and control the Stress factor by telling yourself that you are not going to allow a high level of stress in your life.

Have I confused you yet? I'll explain. Stress is something that we make up in our mind. We make things stressful that may or may not be stress inducing. An event or situation that could stress you out, might not stress someone else out.

As an example, many people stress about getting everything right. Take getting good grades as an example. My daughter, Jaylyn, has always obsessed over her grades. While that wasn't necessarily a bad thing, she would get frustrated and upset when her teacher hadn't yet uploaded an assignment or a test score into the system. While technology is generally a great thing, in Jaylyn's case here, having real-time access to her grades wasn't because she was constantly checking to see her scores, and would be angry if a grade was missing.

For Jaylyn, this situation was stressful because she was allowing herself to get worked up over it. There are plenty of other people who wouldn't think twice about the grades and not having real-time access to scores. The point in sharing this story is that much of this stress stuff is made up in our head.

This was also a topic I discussed during a General Electric Women's Network event where myself and the GE CEO, Larry Culp, were both speakers. Larry had kicked the event off talking about the direction the company was heading and my focus was helping these women leaders continue to move the ball, as the business had faced some uncertainty, and was going through some restructuring across the entire GE portfolio. As part of my talk, I discussed how the most powerful weapon against stress is your ability to choose one thought over the other; to control your attitude and how you deal with outcomes and events that are outside of your control.

Most of the time, stress stems from one of two things: A false time crunch we create due to perceived false deadlines, or because our mind plays tricks on us and makes things more important than they really are, in the grand scheme of things.

Let's discuss the former first. We often create deadlines that aren't critical or real either because we have placed some unnecessary sense of urgency around a due date or because someone has given us an artificial timeline. Now there are circumstances where there are hard and fast deadlines and those are different. But in many cases, there is an arbitrary time limit placed on a task or an activity.

For example, if a co-worker named Joe gives you a task and says, "I need this by Wednesday," what happens if you don't get it done by Wednesday? Would the world end? Would there be some detrimental consequence? Does Joe really need this done by then? Or can it wait until Friday or some other date?

Joe might very well need it by Wednesday, but the point I'm making is that often people come up with a deadline and it's arbitrary. It's the date that Joe wants it but isn't necessarily the date that Joe needs it. If you are already super busy with other tasks, trying to get Joe's task done by his stated deadline might create unnecessary stress in your life. So, what do you do? It's simple. You ask Joe when he really needs this to be complete. This is done by explaining what your other tasks and priorities are and have a conversation around what Joe's true need date is. Then you commit to getting it to him by that date instead of the initial timeline Joe threw at you. By doing this you have eliminated the false time crunch he might have originally put you in.

Something you should do on a weekly basis, at a minimum, is take note of everything you are juggling. Does everything have to get done this week? By managing your game clock and becoming more focused, diligent, and disciplined with how you spend your time, you can control and reduce the amount of stress you are seeing in your life.

The second part of this first principle ties to how our mind tends to place higher importance on things than they really are. For example, you're running around town to get groceries. Yet you're super stressed out about it. There you are sitting in traffic and you're getting all worked up about trying to buy some apples, beef, and broccoli. So now some fruits, meat, and veggies are stressing you out? Don't forget that some people don't even have the luxury of going to the store to get groceries when they want and here you are driving around town, getting to choose what grocery store you want to shop from. Sounds like you have some blessings. Don't lose sight of how you should be suiting up each day with the proper mindset and focusing on how lucky you are.

Here's one more thing to keep in mind: *we create stress and negative energy around the things we don't want to do.* But if you are just willing to give yourself a little dose of perspective, this will help control the stress you are creating in your life.

You might be one of those people thinking that I couldn't possibly understand how busy and hectic your life is. Trust me I do. I raised five children, pretty much as a single parent, worked full-time, and went to school at night for all five of my graduate degrees, and juggled a Fortune 50 career along with serving in the Army National Guard. People often tell me that I'm the busiest person they know, so I really do understand.

When faced with these hectic situations, the first way to control the "S" factor is to gain perspective on the situation. Most of the time, stress is made up by false beliefs and negative self-talk. Limit that.

Principle #2: Control the controllables and practice acceptance.

Plain and simple, there are events and outcomes in your life that are outside of your control. When these types of events happen, it's important to remember that you need to stop focusing on the things you can't control or change, and just *control what you can control.*

This is a common lesson athletes learn playing football and other competitive sports. During a conversation I had with pro wide receiver Jalen McCleskey (son of retired NFL defensive back JJ McCleskey), Jalen discussed with me that Oklahoma State football head coach, Mike Gundy, used to tell them all the time about how they needed to "control what you can control."

For example, if they had an upcoming game and it was supposed to rain, Coach Gundy would tell the players they couldn't control the weather, but what they could do is focus on how they played and to lock in and execute. Jalen took this mentality off the field into everyday life and if there was something he had no control over, there was no point in sulking or stressing about it, because according to Jalen, "it doesn't change the outcome and doesn't make things any better." The lesson here is to realize that you can't control everything that occurs and you shouldn't create stressful events around the things that are outside of your control.

Another common problem is that people hold onto the past and expend energy stressing out over a door that has closed and that feeling of rejection. It's important to recenter and remind ourselves that whatever happened to us is in the past; we should refrain from stressing out or worrying over it. That door is already closed.

Yes, perhaps we wished we still had a relationship with someone, or a potential business opportunity still existed, but the reality is it's gone. So, we need to stop thinking about it and stressing over it. I don't mean to come across as harsh or insensitive, but the reality is we need to accept it and move on. Time does not always heal the pain of a door shutting, but acceptance can, and it's a skill that should be used frequently.

> " Let go of the stuff you can't control and start using your time to master what you can control."—Catherine Goldberg

I want to emphasize that acceptance does not mean you agree with, condone, appreciate, or even like what has transpired. You may also never know why something happened. That's part of the reason we hold onto events because we don't understand the why behind them. While it's nice to know why something occurred, we don't *need* to know the why. We just need to accept the situation for what it is and that's that. You move on.

Acceptance means you know, regardless of the situation, there is something bigger than you at work and that it will be ok. Instead of wasting time and effort on things of the past, recognize it's time to move on and focus your energy on getting through new doors that are opening in front of you. Practice acceptance and let it go.

So that's part of this second way to reduce stress. The other part of this is just focusing on the things you can control and not stressing over the rest. You can't control what other people do or how certain outcomes will turn out, so don't sweat that stuff. I call this control the controllable, which is what you can do. So, when you focus on the things you can control and not worry about the other things, this is another way you will see less stress in your life.

Principle #3: Learn to breathe.

This last one is to learn to breathe. If you can regulate your breath, you can regulate pretty much anything in life. The power of your breath is immense. Your breath is the one element that connects you to the rest of your body, it keeps you alive and helps you navigate the physical and emotional challenges of life. Usually, when you're angry, stressed, or scared, the rhythm of your breath accelerates, sometimes so much that you can hardly articulate a word.

Most of our mental tension stems from our physical tension. If you're not breathing in the moment and you're always taking little sips of air, you are going to deal worse with stress. Allow yourself to just breathe. Let your stomach out and fill it up and expand and contract. When you allow yourself to breathe and breathe deeply, you're going to calm yourself down and relieve the stress that you're feeling. Studies have shown that the deeper breathing you do, the calmer you can make yourself. Give yourself time to take in some more breaths and you'll be more effective at controlling and managing the stress level in your life.

One of the most important decisions you're going to make is how to better handle stress. The time to start that is now. You can't play around with your health and well-being. Stress can do a real number on you. Life is too short to be going through it being stressed all the time. Decide today that you aren't going to subject yourself to unnecessary stress by grabbing a new perspective, controlling the controllable, and just breathe.

COACH'S CHALKBOARD

1. Controlling stress starts with changing your perspective.

2. Make the conscious choice to not be stressed over things that don't really matter.

3. Stop placing false time crunches on tasks or agreeing to arbitrary and artificial deadlines.

4. Acceptance makes it easier to move on from unpleasant events.

5. Regulate your breath and breathe, breathe, breathe.

CHAPTER 20:
CALL THE TIME OUT

"When the game is over, I just want to look at myself in the mirror, win or lose, and know I gave it everything I had."
—Joe Montana

The Chicago Bears and the Green Bay Packers are the oldest rivalry in the NFL, having a history dating back to 1921. While these teams have a storied past, the two have also only played against each other twice in the NFL postseason. The first matchup was the week after the attack on Pearl Harbor on December 14, 1941, where the Bears won 33-14 in a place the Chicago Cubs still call home, Wrigley Field. The second post-season game was the National Football Conference (NFC) Championship Game on January 23, 2011. While I wasn't around to witness the Bears' 1941 victory, the NFC Championship game is one that I recall vividly as I was in the stadium at Soldier Field, freezing my you know what off (in seventeen-degree weather). While the outcome of the NFC Championship game wasn't what I had wanted, this game was always special for me as there was a moment in the game that became the inspiration for my book, *Move the Ball.*

If you've read *Move the Ball,* I go into more details about that game, but the moment that sparked my desire to write the book (and what became the beginning of the Move the Ball movement) was a Chicago Bears' possession in the fourth quarter where the Bears were trying to tie the game. Green Bay was ahead by a touchdown, there were less than two minutes remaining, and while the Bears were struggling, the game and a comeback was still within reach. But then in typical Bears fashion, it quickly became fourth down. It was 4th and 5 to be exact. This was the playoffs, it was a do-or-die situation, the loser went home and that would be the end until next season. The Bears had to go for it.

Lovie Smith, the then Bears' head coach, called a time-out. Why would he do that? Simple. They had a time out and it was a crucial moment. The team needed to regroup and discuss the next play. That's why the time out was used.

Now I wish I had a better story to share here and say that the Bears were able to execute and convert the fourth down, but that isn't what happened. The Packers ended up winning the game, 21-14 at Soldier Field, and then went on to win Super Bowl XLV a couple of weeks later.

While the Bears didn't tie or win the game, the reason I share this story with you is to highlight the importance of taking the time out, which was the right call by Lovie at that moment in the game.

The structure and rules for most sports include each team being allocated time outs because they are an important part of being able to halt the play in a game. It allows coaches and players to communicate with the team, determine strategies and plays, bring some positive energy, inspire morale, or to just stop the game clock.

While time outs are an important part of sports, they are also an important part of life. We need them as they are an effective way to *recharge, reset, refocus, replan, and re-commit*. The beauty about calling timeouts in life is that we don't have a set number unlike in a football or basketball game.

towards those challenging goals you have set for yourself. You can't keep running on an empty tank. It's easy to get to that state whether you are an entrepreneur, or a corporate warrior, but you have to make sure you are calling the time outs when you need them to get re-energized.

Taking a break can also lead to refocusing, resetting, replanning, and discovering breakthroughs. It comes as no surprise to you how difficult, frustrating, and trying life can be. Sometimes we want to throw our hands up and waive the white surrender flag.

Have you ever gone through the morning, nothing is going your way, and things simply fell apart and you wished you could have a restart? I'm talking about one of those days where you just wish you could start the whole day over. When you woke up, it seemed like it was going to be a fantastic day, but then you got derailed or distracted. Perhaps you had a bad interaction with someone, there was a conflict, and now you are feeling bad about the day. You're feeling frustrated and struggling. Yea, do these kinds of days sound familiar?

A lot of people don't have the resiliency to take a time out and restart in the middle of the day, so what happens is they end up just losing the entire day to a bad mood, to bad energy, to bad productivity, and to being ineffective. When it seems like it's going to be the worst day ever, this is the perfect time to step back and pause.

Take a break and ask yourself, *what was I really supposed to do today?* The reason for this question is it's resetting you to become more strategic and deliberate with how you need to spend the rest of your day, instead of being in a reactive mode. Many people react to other people's texts, other people's needs, and other people's emails. They go to work, check their inbox to see what's going on, but all they are doing is being reactive instead of strategic and effective with their time. Or people are in a situation where there is so much coming at them, they are completely overwhelmed because they have no agenda.

By taking a few minutes to remind yourself what your objectives are for the day, it'll allow you to reset, replan, and refocus. Don't forget to breathe, too, while you're taking the time out! Going outside for a walk with your favorite playlist of music for twenty minutes is also a good way to just get away and allow yourself to reset. As you're jamming out to the music, just think about what you are grateful for in your life. Remember, suiting up and showing up in life the right way are largely driven by your perspective.

Then when you're ready to replan and get refocused, ask yourself the following questions:

- *What are my key projects and strategic priorities that I need to work on today, that I need to accomplish today?*

- *What three things still need to be completed today?*

- *Who are the key people I need to contact or I am waiting on?*

- *What information do I need that I don't yet have the answers to?*

- *Who should I collaborate with or interact with so I can move my projects and my priorities forward?*

When you answer these questions, coupled with activating some simple self-talk (as discussed in "Suit Up"), you'll then be back on a path of purpose and you'll be refocused and recommitted to making the rest of your day one that you can claim a success. You'll be ready to win the day and won't have time for drama or distractions. You'll be ready to crush it.

Lastly, if you're taking a time out because you feel as if life is falling apart, think about what kind of reward you'll give yourself for accomplishing the things you need to get done for the day. By giving yourself some sort of treat, you're going to be more energized and enthusiastic about turning your day around and still being able to claim the day as a success.

There you have it—the time out. It's an important element for sports teams to be successful on the field and on the court, and it's a crucial component to dominating the day and winning in life. Work hard, stay focused, but take a vacation when you need to recharge, and call the time outs often when you need to reset, replan, refocus, and recommit so that you can continue to move the ball and win each day.

COACH'S CHALKBOARD

1. Time outs are a necessary part of winning.

2. Take the time outs when you need them.

3. Stop running on an empty tank—make sure you are treating yourself as a priority.

4. Breakthroughs come from breaks.

5. Reset, replan, refocus, and you'll continue to move the ball.

CHAPTER 21:
NEVER TAKE A LOSS

"It's not wanting to win that makes you a winner,
it's refusing to fail."
—Peyton Manning

The "L" word. Nobody likes to hear it, feel it, or see it. On game day, athletes surely don't want to experience it. But just as uncertainty is certain in life, so is the likelihood of losing. Sure, a football team or a basketball team might go undefeated for a season, or longer, but at some point, that L will hit.

When it does, that loss will burn, it will sting, and yes it will hurt. It could even be completely heartbreaking. That's just how life goes sometimes. I know, unfair right?

What's important to remember though is even though an outcome of a game or some event or circumstance in our life results in us not "winning," that doesn't mean we need to take a loss. It's not the result that we need to focus on. Rather, it's what we do because of the situation that matters.

Michael Jordan is unquestionably one of the greatest players to ever play the game. During his 15-season NBA career, Jordan won six championship titles with the Chicago Bulls, was a six-time NBA Finals MVP, five-time NBA Most Valuable Player, and a fourteen-time NBA All-Star. These are just a handful of his countless accomplishments. "MJ," as he was also known, was integral in helping to popularize the

NBA around the globe during the 1980s and 1990s. Because of MJ's on-the-court performances, he became a global icon.

While Jordan has moved the ball in so many ways, he's also missed over 9,000 shots in his career and lost almost 300 games. According to Jordan "26 times I've been trusted to take the game winning shot and missed. I've failed over and over again in my life and that is why I succeed."

> " 26 times I've been trusted to take the game winning shot and missed. I've failed over and over gain in my life and that is why I succeed."
> —Michael Jordan

Jordan experienced repeated failure throughout his career, had multiple losses, and yet managed to be one of the GOATs. Take another basketball great, Kobe Bryant. Kobe missed 14,481 shots, the most ever in NBA history. All on his way to one of the greatest careers in sports. So don't be afraid to miss. Keep shooting!

Failure is a necessary component of success. It's okay to fail and fail often. What's important is we never let those failures become losses, meaning we need to ensure we take the lessons that those events can teach us. Failure is the lesson taught, success is the lesson applied.

Life is based on leverage. The more you know how to leverage it, the more successful you become. This is true when looking at how to strategically play the hand you've been dealt as well as when figuring out your next moves because of an unexpected outcome or a failure.

Remember that success is not always about greatness, but it is about consistency. You need to consistently show up and perform. Sometimes, the outcomes don't pan out the way you want them to.

But that doesn't mean you stop. You don't quit playing the game. You continue on with your plan, apply the lessons, pivot as needed, and keep pushing forward.

As entrepreneurs, as leaders, as players in the game of life, sometimes we feel like we've hit a wall after we have a disappointing moment (that's code word for failure). Then what happens to many people is they simply give up. They feel defeated and they make excuses instead of fighting those limiting beliefs and pressing on. The thing about defeat is it's only bitter if you swallow it. If you learn from it, it's a sweet thing as it provides you with opportunity for growth and for bigger and better experiences to come your way.

A friend of mine, Anthony Trucks, is a motivational speaker, coach, and former NFL player. A fun fact about Anthony is he became the first NFL player to hit the buzzer as a competitor on the hit tv show *American Ninja Warrior*. He's also crushing it in the speaking space and with his coaching programs. When I had Anthony on my *Move the Ball* podcast in June of 2020, a focus of our conversation was on entrepreneurship and how the journey to being a successful entrepreneur is like a roller coaster ride. The highs are incredibly high and the lows, well those are not fun to talk about, but they are distressingly and depressingly low.

On the episode, Anthony shared a saying he loves which is "a smooth sea makes not a skilled sailor." This is essentially saying that if things are easy, you don't learn how to navigate the hardships. Anthony then discussed how he deals with a lot of circumstances that would shut most people down every day. But Anthony is a winner and determined not to ever take a loss.

Whenever Anthony felt like he reached a limit or like life was as piling on was too much, his process was to shift his brain and reframe his thinking. "I have to literally sit there and say, is this truly a limit or is it just hard for me?"

Successful players in the game realize they must learn from situations so they can effectively navigate through it every time the situation pops up. According to Anthony, he has a seven second rule he uses whenever he is dealing with a stressful experience or unexpected outcome. He gives himself seven seconds to wallow in it and just think about it.

After that he's focused on figuring out his next moves. He looks at how can he solve a problem he's facing in his business or how to move on from a setback. The reason he takes seven seconds and then ponders about his next move is because Anthony believes that whatever you go looking for, you'll ultimately find.

Anthony's approach is to always look for solutions before looking for excuses. When he was focused on seeking solutions, his brain was then locked in on finding solutions every single time. As I listened to Anthony sharing his seven-second rule with me on the podcast, at that time I thought about how we were living in unprecedented times with the Coronavirus pandemic. A lot of people made excuses when things didn't turn out in their favor, and they accepted those losses. When outcomes didn't pan out for me, I didn't play the blame game or the victim. I refused to take a loss.

As you already know, a few months before the pandemic, I left my corporate job to go all-in on my business. There is no way I was going to let losses stack up and give up. So, I learned the lessons, sometimes very hard ones so those experiences would not have been for no reason. You know what? I am grateful for each and every one of those experiences.

Look, failing is hard. Not getting the job you want or not winning the game sucks. But the people who succeed in life are not the ones who don't ever falter or fail. They are the ones who, in spite of those setbacks, decide how they are going to keep pursuing their goals. They assess, reflect, and learn from every situation and then they focus on making the next play count.

All successful entrepreneurs, business leaders, and athletes will say you need to fail first and fail often. You just need to make sure you are failing forward and learning from the situations. Failure is not the opposite of success; it is a part of the success. Just like when you were a kid you didn't learn to walk by following some magic rules. You learned by doing and falling over and over. The same is true with anything you are trying to do as an adult.

Thomas Edison, inventor and founder of General Electric, conducted 1,000 failed experiments before discovering the light bulb. Every failed experiment gets you one step closer to success. You will fail at some point in your life, you will embarrass yourself, and you will underperform at something. Embrace it because it's inevitable.

Actors and entertainers don't land gigs all the time. Think about a time when you didn't get that job you wanted. You didn't quit. You didn't fall back and give up. You walked out of that situation ready to prepare for the next one. There's an old saying that if you hang around the barbershop long enough, sooner or later you are going to get a haircut.

When you take the Ls, learn from them, and remain persistent, things will work out in your favor. Doors will open. Results will happen. You have to keep suiting up, showing up, and moving forward. Once again, consistency gets you across the goal line.

Life is always going to be full of obstacles and moments of defeat. It happens to all of us. But once it has occurred, it's in the past. And what happened in your past is not and should not define who you are and where you are going now and in the future. Your potential is reached when you start to do what is uncomfortable. Stretching yourself beyond your current capabilities is going to include disappointment, a season of suck, heartbreak, and growing pains.

If you want to be great though, then it is up to you to never take a loss. Sometimes failure is the best way to figure out where you're going. Never make excuses and never settle from a failure or a misstep. Turn those experiences into lessons and keep pressing forward. That's what winners do and so should you.

COACH'S CHALKBOARD

1. Winners fall. But they always get back up and don't stop until they cross their goal line.

2. Every defeat, every heartbreak, every loss, every closed door provides you with growth.

3. Our obstacles and our failures make us who we are, don't take a loss.

4. When faced with a failure or setbacks, pause, and remember the seven-second rule.

5. Failure is a lesson learned; success is a lesson applied.

CHAPTER 22:
MOVE THE BALL

"It's not so important who starts the game but who finishes it."
—John Wooden

Average people have great ideas. Legends have great execution. Being extraordinary is all about the execution. Great leaders know how to execute. Phenomenal athletes know how to make plays happen.

Throughout this book, I've given you different principles and strategies to suit up, to show up, to remain focused, to be effective, and to move the ball. Here are a few other rules to remember as you continue to move forward towards accomplishing your goals and living that life that you want and that you deserve.

Rule #1: The speed doesn't matter, forward is forward.

It is so easy for us to get caught up in the fact that things don't happen as quickly as we want them to. It's been mentioned already that greatness doesn't happen overnight. Successes don't occur instantaneously. You might have heard the saying *don't compare your Chapter 1 to someone else's Chapter 20*. In today's day, social media tends to discourage us because we compare ourselves to what we see online, their accomplishments, and the lifestyle they get to live.

What we fail to realize is what we see is only what people want us to see. Meaning that it's a filtered glimpse of their life. They don't show you all the struggles and the challenges they go through to be able to post "the good stuff" about their life. The other thing you also have to remember is that everyone has their own path and their journey.

Some people are born into wealthy families and already have connections and a network to help them accelerate their business opportunities on Day 1. There are also individuals who are single, have no children, and don't have to worry about anyone but themselves. Then there are some who are married with kids, there are single parents out there, and there are others who are having to care for aging parents. The situations I could come up with are endless and the point is, we are all different and we all have distinct circumstances we are dealing with in life. So, you cannot compare yourself to other people's progress and where they are in life. Some of those people started working on their success 10 years before you.

As discussed earlier in this book, you need to focus on your path and not compare yourself to others. That comparison game distorts your ability to see the good you are doing. It derails you from focusing on what you can control. Comparison will rob your happiness and impede you from what matters most: *developing into the best version of yourself and achieving what you want in life.*

If you must move slower toward your goals, there is nothing wrong with that. This whole Move the Ball movement I created was simply about forward motion. It's about taking effective and purposeful action to make forward progress. Whether that ball gets moved an inch, a foot, a yard, or you get a first down or score a touchdown. No matter how slow or how fast... forward is forward, progress is progress. When you show up and consistently take action, that's when you will see the outcomes you want in life. Keep in mind too that if you're focused on moving forward, even if it's at a slower pace, you're still lapping those who are stuck on their couch (or the sideline, to tie it back to a sports metaphor).

Rule #2: Commitment & Consistency are essential parts of the playbook.

If you're going to set high goals for yourself, you must consider the lifestyle it's going to require in order to achieve those goals. Remember you can't commit to the destination if you're not willing to commit to the process required to get you there. Being "all in" as discussed in "Own Your Game" requires you to be committed to the game you're playing, committed to the process, and committed to being consistent daily. Without commitment you will never start, but it's without consistency that you will never finish.

With the professional athletes and high performers that I work with, something we always come back to is the important of showing up *and* being consistent. That's why they are themes used in this book. They are necessary components to winning.

As an example, in the NFL, 1% of all college football players get drafted to play at that level. While it's hard to get into the NFL, it's even harder to stay in the NFL with the average NFL career spanning only about 2.5 years. A player can be great on one play, maybe two plays, but they have to be able to do it the rest of the game. They must consistently perform day in and day out, because if they don't, there's someone else waiting to take their spot. So that consistency in their daily practices is critical for longevity in their professional football career.

The same is true for all of us, corporate professionals, entrepreneurs, business leaders, professional athletes, or some other profession. When you look at how people show up every day, what really separates those elite people from others out there is they are consistent in performing at how they need to perform.

Rule #3: Your journey is an evolution.

Part of embracing the process is understanding that no matter how focused you are or how hard you work, you can't force how fast the results come. "Trust the Process" emphasized the importance of this and managing your emotions as things unfold when results aren't lining up with your expectations. You cannot get caught up when things are not working according to your desired timeline.

Keep in mind too, that as you continue to improve and evolve on your journey, your process should also evolve. Just because something is working for you now (or has worked for you previously), doesn't mean it's going to continue to work for you in the future. Additionally, something that didn't work for you in the past, doesn't mean that it can't work for you now.

In life, we are always having to pivot and make adjustments if we want to continue to get across the goal line. The road to success is rarely ever a straight line and there'll be speed bumps, curves, roadblocks, and so much more along the way. You have to make turns as you need to so you can keep things moving and ultimately arrive at your destination. Keep adjusting, evolving, and pivoting as necessary.

Rule #4: Focus on the next play.

This mentality is something that I, along with the professional athletes I work with, discuss all the time. As an example, defensive backs sometimes get beat out on the football field. They miss a tackle which results in their opponent making a big catch or even scoring a touchdown. When that happens, they just have to let that play get out of their head and focus on getting back in the game and concentrating on the next one.

As human beings, we are not perfect. We make mistakes, we have missteps, and sometimes we drop or fumble the ball. Sometimes we fall short of our own expectations at times. There are moments where we will fail in things that we are "supposed" to be able to do. This is all normal and part of life. When this happens, you need to forgive yourself quickly, forgive others, learn the lesson, and move on.

Rule #5: Learn from your experiences and others too.

Life is a teacher. Each day it presents you with opportunities to learn something new. Whether it be in your career, your educational endeavors, or your personal life, the knowledge you gain from these experiences is invaluable. However, the lessons should not stop there. Learning is a gift and you should continually look for the teachings as you push yourself along on life's journey—embracing every moment of discomfort and maintaining the courage to push through those times of uncertainty, apprehension, and feeling uncomfortable.

During Season 3 of the *Move the Ball* podcast, I did an episode with NFL linebacker Zaire Franklin who played college football at Syracuse and was a three-time team captain in college, making him the second person in Syracuse history to do so and the first since 1896. Zaire was drafted by the Indianapolis Colts in the 2018 NFL Draft and has also served as a captain on the team. As part of our conversation, I asked Zaire what some of the strategies and lessons he had learned from football were that have helped him to be successful.

He answered by first saying that it was the ability to assess every situation, whether good or bad, learn from it, and then move on from it. This is something he felt most people didn't do. With every experience, it's essential to take what's needed to learn from it, whether it's a victory or not, get the lesson, and move on. Psst...this concept should be familiar to you as it was also discussed in "Never Take a Loss."

Zaire also shared the importance of watching other's mistakes and learning from those so you don't repeat those type of things. When it came to football, he would learn from the guy in front of him and pick up on what that person was doing wrong. As he said:

> *"In the NFL, you come to learn that reps are scarce, especially as a seventh-round pick. I was like the 11th draft pick that year and the last guy that they got in. I wasn't*

getting as many reps. So I knew when I got out there, I had to really maximize my opportunity. So one of the biggest things for me was just really watching and learning from the guys ahead of me, learning what they did good and learning from what they did bad. So I didn't make similar mistakes."

The takeaway here is to make sure you are continually reviewing and assessing your experiences, taking lessons from all of them, as well as learning from others' successes and mistakes so that you can continue to improve and make the progress you need to each day.

Rule #6: Finish.

This rule is about one simple word: *finish*. While it's something straightforward, this is where so many people fall short. If you want to move the ball, you've got to finish those necessary tasks and activities you start. Take writing this book as an example. I needed to finish my outline, finish writing each chapter, finish the cover design, etc. But guess what? I completed all those things. Yes, of course I did, or else you wouldn't be reading this right now.

Let's go with another example. Steven Parker II is an NFL defensive back who played college football at Oklahoma and signed as an undrafted free agent with the Los Angeles Rams. Some other teams Steven has played with include the Miami Dolphins, the Minnesota Vikings, the New York Giants, and the Washington Commanders.

For Steven, one of the habits he learned from being a competitive athlete is the importance of needing to finish. Coaches are always preaching "finish, finish, finish the rep, finish the set…" Steven shared with me that "everything we do in life, we have to finish. If you go halfway and the finish line is just a couple of feet away, then you almost just failed yourself because you're looking right there at the end of the tunnel, and you didn't put forth the effort in order to just get it done. So, you have to finish and make sure that you see it all the way through."

This concept of finishing is something other athletes know the importance of as well. This is something two-time WNBA champion, Olympia Scott, and I have talked about multiple times and something she also shared about when she joined me on my show during Season 1 of the *Move the Ball* podcast.

Whatever it is you set out to do, make sure you finish. 99% of people give up inches before the goal line. Don't be one of them. Finish what you need to, remain persistent, and the outcomes will happen.

Of course, I'll share another example to keep you motivated. The date was October 23, 2000, and an evening where many, especially New York Jets fans, consider to be the greatest Monday Night Football game. Playing in the Meadowlands that Monday evening were the Jets and the Miami Dolphins. With Miami leading 30–7 early in the fourth quarter, the crowd was starting to thin. But something I learned as a young girl watching football games is the game isn't over until it's over and a principle I wrote about in *Move the Ball* was the need to "play the full 60."

Despite being down twenty-three points, the Jets were not ready to throw in the towel. I'm sure Jets fans would be pretty pissed if they had been. After all, those guys on the field are professional football players, they get paid handsomely to play competitive football, and fans expect them to continue to play the game.

And play is what they did. They were committed to finishing this game. In the fourth quarter, quarterback Vinny Testaverde hit Laveranues Coles with a 30-yard touchdown pass followed by another throw to Jermaine Wiggins with a 1-yard touchdown pass. Suddenly the game was now 30–20. Jets kicker, John Hall, then kicked a 34-yard field goal, and fans watching in the stadium and on television found themselves with a seven-point game with more than five minutes to go. The scoring continued and Wayne Chrebet's 24-yard touchdown catch tied the game with 3 minutes and 55 seconds left in the game.

The Dolphins responded with a 46-yard touchdown pass from Jay Fiedler. But wait, there's more. Testaverde, who would finish the night 36-for-59 for 378 yards and 5 TDs, hit Jumbo Elliott with a three-yard touchdown pass with 42 seconds left in the game. They went into overtime where John Hall kicked the game winning field goal.

There you have it. The Jets had pulled off a miracle comeback because they were committed to showing up, executing on each play, not giving up, and focused on finishing. You can't underestimate the power of persistence, especially in the game of life.

In life you have the luxury that you don't have a 60-minute game clock you are playing up against. So, you can keep playing until you have finished what you need to so you can get across your goal line and win.

As you've heard time and time again, there is no such thing as an overnight success. There also is no great story where the main character didn't overcome massive adversity. Instead of wishing that your life was easier, remember the hard makes you great. There is power in understanding that pain is part of the process and failing is part of the journey. Choosing the easy road doesn't lead to growth, it leads to mediocrity. It's not about avoiding the struggle, it's about developing the ability to thrive in it. We're all built through adversity and it's those experiences that define us and help prepare us for the next level of greatness. You've got to keep playing the game, continue to show up and one day, you'll look back at how far you come and be glad that you didn't give up.

COACH'S CHALKBOARD

1. Forward is forward, the speed doesn't matter.

2. Don't expect to be great if you're not willing to keep going when times get tough.

3. You give power to what you focus on.

4. Consistency is what transforms average into excellence.

5. Forget the last play, learn the lesson. Move on.

6. Finish. Just finish.

CHAPTER 23:
PLAY ON PLAYER

"Remember, tomorrow is promised to no one."
—Walter Payton

Tomorrow is an interesting word. It's an eight-letter term we often use when mentioning or thinking about the things we don't want to do today.

"I'll just take care of that tomorrow." That's what we say to ourselves or to other people, never thinking about whether tomorrow will come. We just take the day for granted.

If there is something I have come to appreciate because of my dad's unexpected passing, it's that tomorrow is as uncertain as the outcome of a football game. You never know what the next day will bring or whether there will be a next day at all. As said before, *tomorrow is never guaranteed.*

Therefore, we cannot wait until tomorrow to start the journey towards happiness. We must start living our best life today. This needs to be the beginning of a brand new you, someone who is fully committed to dominating the game. Because you have made it through to this chapter, I know you are ready to make the changes required to achieve your goals. While life will continually push back on you, it's so important that you suit up and show up ready to push forward in life. It's time to step out of your confines of comfortability and have the courage to play your game in a way that will stretch, challenge, test, and grow you.

If there is something I have learned through building and growing the Move the Ball movement, it is this: *Just be yourself. Life is too short to be someone else.* Your past doesn't define you or limit where you are going, but it's your experiences that have made you who you are today. Be proud of that, no matter what you have gone through. I thought I had to hide different parts of my story, of my struggle, of who I was, and of who I wanted to be. But I was wrong. When I started sharing more of those things, doors of opportunity opened.

I remember all the "No's" I got along my journey and the people who told me I was wasting my time with the Move the Ball movement and wanting to work with professional athletes. Not everyone is meant to be on the journey with you. Stop listening to others. Stop letting them define who you are and who you can become. Stop letting them determine your worth. That is for you and only you to decide.

Start by clarifying your values and getting clear around your purpose. What color is your jersey? What is the *why* behind everything that you do? Fulfilling your purpose is the most rewarding thing you can do in life. You owe that to yourself.

Stop settling for less than what you deserve. Stop letting anyone discourage you from showcasing your true self. Stop letting other people determine your potential. Be proud of who you are. When you don't care about what other people say, and you have let go of that fear of judgment, you have reached a dangerously amazing level of freedom.

When you unleash who you truly are, that is when you can focus on bringing a better version of yourself into each day. That is when you can perform at your highest and serve others at your best. That is when you separate yourself from the average player and really start to become great.

It's important for you to understand what game you are playing. You might know what jersey you are wearing, but have you defined your game? Understanding that is critical. This is your time to decide what is important to you and what will bring you joy. You need to know this for the short-, medium-, and long-term. Your priorities will change over time, so adjust as needed and ensure that your goals and the game you are playing are always in alignment with your assignment and with what you want.

Succeeding in life requires having an edge over others—how you choose to suit up and show up will determine the outcomes that you have in life. Great athletes train for every game, with a proactive strategy and with purpose so they can dominate it. From the moment they step onto the field, they are mentally, physically, and emotionally ready to win. They bring the mental toughness and are locked in on handling their business.

Now it's your turn to enter the stadium. This book has prepared you to dominate your own game. Whether you are successful now depends on you. Look in the mirror. Have you been making your goals your main focus? If you haven't, the time to start is now.

First, you need to commit to this journey and take ownership over your life. Winning involves an intense focus on the things that are most important to you. Are you willing to put in the hard work and sacrifice that is required?

You're not always going to be in the most motivated frame of mind. So, plan ahead and that discipline is what is going to keep you going. Make it easy for yourself by sticking to a morning routine, removing distractions, and managing your game clock. Win every day by playing your game with intention. Not just taking what shows up. Drive how each day will end.

This ride will try your patience, I'm not going to tell you it won't. Beating life's challenges is not stress-free and it requires you to control the "S" factor and to push yourself into uncomfortable and unfamiliar territory. Old practices won't get you to where you want to go. Changing some of your behaviors is necessary. You need to ditch those old clothes and break through old habits if you want to unleash your potential and discover new possibilities.

Second, you need to get inside the huddle. Defining your goals starts with you but achieving them doesn't happen only because of you. Rarely do people succeed alone. Surround yourself with a team that will support you. Not only do you need people who are affirming and encouraging, you need people who have accomplished what you are looking to achieve, as well as people who will challenge your thinking and enable your growth. They will also keep you grounded, hold you accountable, and accelerate your progress.

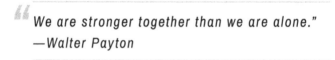

We are stronger together than we are alone."
—Walter Payton

Third, you need to be the quarterback of your destiny and your happiness. You are here to play your game with a pocket presence that is fueled by a higher level of confidence and courage. Keep in mind that the goal is succeeding in the long term. This is not about playing in survival mode, but rather being deliberate and architecting your future by possessing an "always first class" mentality. Players in the 1% always strive for excellence.

Remember that no matter what obstacles may surface, you need to stay strong and locked in. As the quarterback in the game, you get to drive the ball movement. Take ownership, play to your standards, and hold yourself accountable.

Throughout this book, I have provided examples and stories of individuals and teams who have fought through adversity, have been the underdog or underrated, and who have persevered through their situations and won. A common factor in these stories is their consistency in showing up the right way, not being distracted by the noise and the negativity, trusting the process, and possessing a relentless work ethic. To be successful, your work ethic must match the dream.

Champions in life and in sports inspire and motivate themselves to always persevere. That's what you need to do too. Like it or not, we need challenges in our lives to value our accomplishments. We thrive on the feelings of overcoming hurdles. When you get knocked down, you need to rise back up. *Fall seven times, stand up eight.*

As you are getting ready to train for greatness, make sure you have suited up and are mentally prepared to go after what you want in life. A lot of the professional athletes I work with talk about how succeeding in their sport is largely mental. The same is true off the field. As the corporate executives and entrepreneurs who I also coach will say, having mental toughness gives you an edge and separates you from the norm. Others will cave at the sight of challenge, but you are different. You're going to stay focused and will show up and cross your goal line. Always remain connected to your purpose as it will give you the strength to continue to push on through times of adversity.

Congratulations, you've made it through this book. Now it's time for you to write a life's story that you never want to stop reading. Remember, it's not how you start, it's how you finish. It's not about how slow or how fast you go, as long as you are consistent, and you don't give up. When you commit to consistency your hard work will lead you to success and to a victory formation. Don't wait until you reach your goal to be proud of yourself. Look back at where you came from and let yourself feel good about your progress. Hold yourself accountable and live with a "no excuses" mindset. Make each day count. They are not unlimited.

Life is short. Time is fast. There is no DVR for this game called life. You cannot pause it, rewind it, or replay it. Tomorrow is never promised or guaranteed. So, starting today, play your game with intention. Focus your time, energy, and efforts on the things that matter, on the relationships you value, and just be you. People who walk in purpose don't have to chase people or opportunities. Their light causes people and opportunities to pursue them.

Always remember that you matter. You are beautiful. You are amazing. You are capable. Lastly, you are unstoppable. Today is day one of the new you. Get out there—*suit up* with the right preparation and mindset, then *show up* in every single moment like you are supposed to be there. You've got this! It's your time to make things happen, so play on player. Until you cross that goal line, make sure you dominate the game and that every day you suit up, you show up, and you move the ball.

JEN'S NOTES

We all know how you show up to life matters. While conceptually we get this, life can be life. It can be hard. It can be harsh. It can be heavy. It can be heartbreaking. Sometimes when life places us in unpleasant and hurtful situations, it can be challenging for us to remain in a positive and hopeful frame of mind.

The notes that I've chosen to share with you on the following pages are thoughts I wrote to myself when I was not at my best. I'm human too and these heart-felt pieces were words I captured to always serve as a reminder to me that no matter the circumstances I was going though, I could and I would make it through by continuing to be true to myself and showing up in a way that would keep me moving forward.

I hope you find these messages encouraging and that they also motivate you to write similar notes to yourself.

NOTE 1:

Being able to move the ball and succeed in life is about controlling what you can control.

I cannot always control the things that happen around me nor can I control other's actions or how people may treat me.

But what I can do is this...

I can always take control and ownership of how I choose to show up in life. I may not be perfect in the things I do, but I'm going to own every single action and I will keep moving forward.

I will not let the distractions of the day-to-day stop me from making the most of each and every day. No matter what.

I will not let any pain I'm feeling hinder my ability to remain mentally locked in and handle my business.

I will learn from and apply the lessons that life wants to teach me.

I will suit up mentally and physically ready to play my game and be the best version of "me" that I can be.

I will trust the process, never doubting it or myself regardless of the outcomes that happen along the way.

I will tune out all of the noise and I will stay in my zone.

I will prove the doubters wrong.

I will show up in the moments like I deserve to be there.

I will move the ball.

NOTE 2:

No matter how much I might be hurting because of someone or something that has happened in my life, my promise to the world will always be this:

Every single day, I will suit up with a mindset that is full of gratitude and be appreciative that I have been blessed and given another day.

Every single day, I will commit to being a better person.

Every single day, I will show up with a smile on my face and shine brightly to light up those around me.

Every single day, I will love others and always be kind for we know the world certainly needs more of it.

Every single day, I will vibrate higher than and above the noise and the negativity that was trying to dial down my ambition.

Every single day, I will strive to make the world a better place and be the example that I want to see.

Every single day, I will be that person that is there for others and lets them know that everything is going to be all right.

Every single day, I will be fully present in every moment and show up in those moments like I am supposed to be there.

Every single day, I will suit up, I will show up, and I will move the ball. No matter what.

NOTE 3:

When life gives you a reason to cry, show life that you have so many other reasons to smile.

No matter how much you might have been hurt by someone or how bad the struggle may seem, know that every storm runs out of rain, just like every dark night turns into day.

Know that you are enough, you are strong enough, and that your darkest nights will produce the brightest stars.

While things may seem unsettling right now, what you are going through doesn't determine or define who you are. It prepares you for who you are meant to be.

If you need to let those tears flow, then let them fall. That doesn't mean you don't have strength; it is a way to cope so that you can carry on and be strong. Remember that sometimes the strongest people in the mornings are the ones who cried all night.

Keep walking through the storm, your rainbow is waiting on the other side.

NOTE 4:

I choose to live my life by always taking ownership and never having a victim mentality. I am not what has happened to me, but I am who I have chosen to become.

The person I am today is because of all of the experiences that I have been through, the good and especially the bad.

While people will reach out and tell me how much they admire what I've accomplished and by my strength, the thing is, being strong doesn't mean you don't get knocked down, get hurt, or ever fall. It just means you have the courage to get back up, each and every time.

A strong person isn't someone who doesn't cry. We cry in silence. We shed those tears for a moment (sometimes two or three) and then we wipe up those tears and dry those eyes. We pick ourselves back up. Then we get ready to face another day.

Always remember that it's not the hurtful events and failures in our lives that define us, it's the moments we decide that getting back up is all that matters.

You can and will get through anything you are facing. Trust in your faith and no matter how dark things may seem, the sun will rise again, I promise.

NOTE 5:

The most impactful moments in my life, the ones where I have experienced the deepest pain, have driven periods of intense reflection and have also provided the most clarity on where I need to go in life and how to continue to move the ball.

God doesn't give his hardest battles to his toughest soldiers, he creates his toughest soldiers out of life's hardest battles.

When you feel incredible pain, ask God to give you strength to endure any situation and to find the blessings and the lessons that that situation contains.

If you need to cry, go ahead and cry. Don't be afraid of those tears. It's part of the journey, so let them flow.

Then what you need to do is trust the process, always walk in faith, and believe that the right things are going to happen. No matter how much pain you might be going through, remember that you are exactly where you are meant to be. God is aligning you to be on the right path and things will be so much clearer soon.

A strong person isn't someone who never cries or experiences anger or sadness. A strong person is the one who cries, sheds tears or does whatever is needed for the moment, then gets up and keeps fighting again. Keep going and don't give up.

And if you need a scoop of ice-cream to help make it a little easier, that's ok. Go ahead and indulge, you deserve it.

Thank you for reading these notes and letting me share them with you. I hope you have found them inspiring. Remember that every experience you go through, every lesson you learn is there by design. Trust the process, fall in love with the process, and know that your faith will get you through everything you might be wrestling with and trying to overcome. There is a purpose for your pain, a reason for your struggle, and a reward for your faithfulness.

You are exactly where you are meant to be and keep doing what you need to do. Faith over fear, always. You will move the ball and dominate your game.

ABOUT THE AUTHOR

Jennifer A. Garrett is an internationally recognized business and branding consultant, entrepreneur, podcast host, best-selling author, and speaker who is widely known for going against the grain and pushing boundaries. She is the founder of the Move the Ball movement, which influences, inspires, and empowers individuals to go after the opportunities, careers, and lifestyles that they want and deserve.

Jennifer holds herself to a high standard and isn't afraid to show up to life and tackle any challenge or obstacle that she might face. Jennifer, herself, has been a teenage single parent, navigated a military career, played in multiple male-dominated industries, dealt with entitled employees, and built a well-respected brand in professional sports from scratch, starting with no connections in the industry.

Jennifer's organization Elevate Your Hustle, LLC works with corporations, business executives, and professional athletes on how to create and position their brands to attract incredible opportunities, drive business growth, and reach that next level of success. Jennifer pushes people out of their comfort zones, helps them solve their biggest challenges, and coaches teams how to play "on offense", elevate their productivity, and dominate the game. She draws upon her experience working in multiple Fortune 50 companies where she led multi-billion-dollar campaigns and quarterbacked complex commercial transactions.

Jennifer currently serves in the U.S. military as an Army Judge Advocate and holds seven college degrees. They are as follows: Bachelor of Science (B.S.) in Electrical Engineering, B.S. in Biomedical and Clinical Engineering, Master of Business Administration (MBA), Master of Arts (M.A.) in Communication and Leadership Studies, Juris Doctor (J.D.), Master of Laws (LL.M.) in Business Transactions, and LL.M. in Taxation.

Jennifer worked full-time while pursuing each of her graduate degrees and raising her five children. In her spare time, Jennifer enjoys watching sports, with her true passions being football and basketball. She also enjoys traveling with her family.

You can connect with Jennifer in the following ways:

- *Learn More About Jennifer and How She Can Help You: www.getinsidethehuddle.com*

- *Connect with Jennifer on LinkedIn: www.linkedin.com/in/movetheball/*

- *Follow Jennifer on Instagram: @movetheball*

- *Follow Jennifer on Twitter: @getintheendzone*

- *Follow Jennifer on TikTok: @movetheballpodcast*

- *Join Jennifer's Mailing List: www.thenextfirstdown.com*

- *Listen to the Move the Ball Podcast: www.movetheballpodcast.com*

- *Get your Move the Ball Merchandise: www.wemovetheball.com*

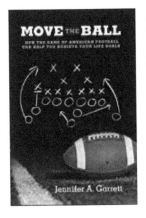

Move the Ball is a book that draws parallels between American football and life; the principles needed to win the game of football are the same principles needed to win the game of life. In both settings, players need to define the goals, develop the playbook, and execute the plays. *Move the Ball* draws upon the football playbook to show you how to be successful. Walk into any bookstore or search online retailers and you'll find numerous books comparing running a business to a team sport. Most of these books concentrate on how to be a good leader, how to gain market share, and how to differentiate your business. *Move the Ball* is different because it's not about your business or your career. It's about you, the whole person. It looks at you, the individual, in ways that speak to the core of who you are. It will challenge you to find your identity and your vision. It will get you off the sideline and help you move the ball. Pick up your copy of *Move the Ball* on Amazon.com today!

Are you ready to think and execute like a pro athlete so that you can elevate your business, career, or personal life? On the *Move the Ball* podcast, Jennifer has conversations with professional athletes, very accomplished entrepreneurs, and Fortune 500 C-suite executives on business, branding, leadership, career, and sports industry topics. These discussions will help you utilize the same tools and strategies as the world's best players and corporate leaders to excel and dominate the game. You can listen to the *Move the Ball* podcast on your favorite podcast platform (Amazon Music, Audible, iHeartRadio, Spotify, Apple Podcasts, etc.) and also at www.movetheballpodcast.com